Pippa ... n
the cou... a
teacher ... t
Stephen ...
had bec... and
where th... for thirteen years, bringing up two
sons. Since the book was written, Stephen has
begun training for full-time ministry. This has
meant the family moving from Toxteth for the
moment, but they do not know where they may be
called to serve in the future.

Down Granby Street

A CHRISTIAN FAMILY IN TOXTETH

Pippa West

TRIANGLE

First published 1988
Triangle
SPCK
Holy Trinity Church
Marylebone Road
London NW1 4DU

British Library Cataloguing in Publication Data

West, Pippa, *1952–*
    Down Granby Street : A Christian family
in Toxteth.
    1. Merseyside (Metropolitan County).
Liverpool. Toxteth. Social life, ca.
1974–1987. Personal observations
    I. Title
942.7'53

ISBN 0–281–04357–4

Photoset by Inforum Ltd, Portsmouth
Made and printed in Great Britain by
Hazell Watson & Viney Limited
Member of BPCC plc
Aylesbury Bucks

Contents

Some of the people who appear in this book have had their names altered or have been otherwise disguised in order to protect their identity.

1
Toxteth by Default

We find ourselves in Granby more or less by default. These days, since the riots of 1981, I make a point of answering 'Toxteth' to people who ask where we live. It's interesting to observe the varied reactions. Before 1981, we simply lived in Liverpool 8 (which was notorious enough then, to anyone in the know). Suddenly in the Eighties the media latched on to Toxteth, and now everyone has heard of us. And we found ourselves in the epicentre of the disturbances.

When I say that we find ourselves here 'by default', I don't mean that we had intended to be elsewhere, or that it was some kind of mistake. We came to live here in 1974, when we married, as part of God's direction for our life together, and we haven't yet been directed elsewhere. We made no conscious decision to Move Into the Inner City, it just happened to be where our church and my husband's job were.

If someone had said to me then that in twelve or thirteen years time I should still be living, and raising a family, in the heart of Toxteth, I would have laughed or panicked or revolted, or all three. I'm not sure what alternative I would have had in mind, but the option of staying wouldn't have figured in my calculations then.

Younger, fresh from college, the world seemed at our feet, and I was ambitious for God. Settling in a small terraced house to be an ordinary family doing ordinary things didn't seem to me to be ambitious in any sense.

When we were at college, many students lived around the Liverpool 8 area. Property was cheap to rent, and student flats passed on to the next generation of students.

1

That was when I first heard of Granby Street. Friends assured me that it was The Place to do your shopping – full of exotic vegetables, fruits and spices, and a visually exciting place to be, a rich blend of cultures and colours and languages.

I didn't get to know it then, but it had a kind of fascination for me. At that time I didn't know anything (not in any depth, anyway) of the grimmer side of life, of the frustrations and futility many of its residents experienced, of the seeds of anger sown into those whose experience seems to demonstrate that they'll always be at the bottom of the pile.

It's very important for me to remember that I didn't choose to be here, because it's sometimes tempting to act as if we've done something sacrificial or noble. That temptation may arise when people from elsewhere learn that we live in Toxteth. Sometimes I hear them thinking, 'What? Nice, middle-class people like you – why on earth do you live there?' And they ask if I like being here, and if it's as bad as the media make out. Usually this is prompted by a healthy interest; occasionally it's a kind of voyeurism. And we discuss their more pleasant lot, and they feel almost apologetic, and I sigh and envy them their garden – or whatever – and they praise my fortitude, and I feel very spiritual.

There are subtler attitudes at work also – a kind of inverted glamour can assert itself. So, notes are compared on the relative awfulness of our respective environments. They have to refuse invitations to wife-swapping parties, we, invitations to buy drugs on the street corner; they have to cope with the grossness of opulence, we, the stench of rotting garbage in the entries; they with the unloved rich children with £20 weekly pocket money, we, with the neglected children who throw bricks at buses – and so on . . .

It's just another form of the game 'My lot's harder than your lot'. Always seeing things from *my* perspective, conscious only of *my* hurts, *my* unfulfilled needs and desires, and not trying to stand in the shoes of my sister or brother for a little while.

Once out of Toxteth, I seem to blot the place out of my immediate consciousness. On holiday people often say, 'Ah, but there's no place quite like home – the best bit of the holiday is coming home again.' I hope they forgive my singularly unenthusiastic responses – but in all honesty, the worst part for me, every time, is coming home again.

For Stephen and me, it's always a silent taxi ride from the station to the corner of our street. Silent, because I'm invariably fighting back the tears as the desert of the inner city assails my senses once again, my immunity having broken down while I was out of it for a while. I forget too easily – breathing in fresh air, smelling the vegetation, touching trees and flowers like a child and pretending it's all mine. And not fearing to carry a bag with me; glad to greet strangers that I pass. I don't want to spoil it all by thinking of my city. Or of the thousands who, unlike me, don't get an annual fortnight in the country – maybe the odd day out, if they're lucky. So that the environment eventually starves them of any sense of the beauty of the world that God created for us to inhabit.

You well may ask why on earth Stephen and I and Thomas and Alexis live in an environment which apparently causes us distress. Because we're Christians, we want to know and respond to God's plan for our lives. Over the years I've been constantly challenged about discerning the will of God. In fact, it has all been quite simple. The bottom line for me is to be here, in Toxteth.

Essentially it's as simple as that, but I've managed to make it pretty hard for myself (and God) a lot of the time. I've argued – with myself, my husband and with God – about our being here. I've found (in the past) guidance to suggest that they (Stephen and God) had got it wrong, and that it was, after all, time to move (to somewhere 'nicer'). I have found it

3

all too easy to listen to the many over the last twelve years who have thought that it's been time for us to move on; we'd done our bit, we owed it to ourselves, we owed it to the children.

No one has 'forced' me to remain. For a long time Stephen was made to feel guilty (largely through me, but also through one or two well-meaning friends and relations) about making me stay here against my will, leaving him torn between his obedience to God and his love for me. He knew with total conviction that being here, remaining here, was right for us. It's not as if it's been a picnic for him either. He is every bit as distressed, for example, as I am at violence. During the various disturbances over the years, not all of which have rated national news coverage by any means, he has been out on the streets in the day or through the night with other local Christian men, observing, seeking wherever possible to be peacemakers and, above all, praying.

He too would like a garden and space – and his need for space is probably greater than mine. He unwinds best in solitude. He has, as a teacher, school work to mark and, as a lay reader in our church, sermons to prepare.

Nor has God, for his part, forced me to stay. Here's a Christian paradox: true freedom is found in obedience. Freedom is to do God's will. I am free to go, and free to stay. For now, we choose the latter, because we remain convinced that it is God's will for us to do so.

2

Choices

Our first home was full of character. Character Number One was Mrs Groves, our landlady. She lived downstairs and we lived upstairs in her dark brown, unrenovated house.

Sometimes we invited her up for tea and scones (if the oven was functioning properly – it blew up from time to time). She reminisced about her days in Burma with her husband (who'd died some years previously). He was 'in rubber'.

Her attitude to black people had been formed in those colonial days, and could only be described nowadays as blatantly racist. Although my own attitudes were still taking shape – like so many, I'd grown up in an all-white community and was therefore ignorant (in all senses) of the true nature of racism in the UK – I felt distinctly uncomfortable at her jokes. No doubt much of it *was* said tongue-in-cheek, and she would have considered it all quite harmless, but I squirm now to think how I listened politely, and remained silent. She was a lonely old soul, and probably deliberately manufactured her eccentric reputation.

Someone didn't appreciate her jests, because as we lay asleep in the bedrooms at the back of the house, bricks would sometimes crash through the windows, landing more than once dangerously close to Mrs Groves' bed. It eventually quite shattered her nerves. However fast we leapt out of bed and over to the window, we never saw anyone. We chicken-wired our windows – hardly surprisingly, not a very effective measure. But we became used to it, and it was all quite cosy and chintzy.

When we first moved in, newly-wed and broke, we had

everything *except* the kitchen sink. So we stacked the washing up in the bath, washed it in the hand basin, and drained it on the lavatory seat.

The bath had character, too. It took a long time for the water to heat up, and a very long time to fill up. On one occasion I had to dash back to fetch something I'd left in the city centre. There was time for a swift ride there and back while the water dribbled in. I got back home to find the bath only just about full.

It all seems so idyllic, looking back, but of course, it didn't always feel like that at the time. I wasn't working, and eventually began to feel lonely – we didn't have our own front door, or back yard, and I felt cut off from the community. A small taste of what thousands experience without hope of a reprieve – especially the elderly, or those whose first language isn't English, or the many in high-rise blocks.

In time we wanted children and decided to buy a house. The building society almost pleaded with me to buy a house *anywhere* else: 'We'll give you a much bigger mortgage – but *please* don't ask us to give you a mortgage in Liverpool 8.' In the end we gave up on the building societies, and, by a series of events little short of miraculous, secured a mortgage from the city council. I think they got tired of finding me outside the doors at nine o'clock every morning.

Both our families had hoped we'd be saying goodbye to the area, so we had moving cards printed, announcing that we were moving south. One hundred yards south in fact, to the next street, and our own front door. Two thieving kittens, called Fortnum and Mason because they ate the cheapest cat food, joined us. The kids in the street called them Fortmin and Basin. A year later our eldest son, Thomas, was born.

So, having established ourselves as a family, we got on with life in the normal way. I stayed at home and looked after Thomas while Stephen taught at the local school. You could say that we were an ordinary family, no better off than any of our neighbours, and materially this may have been true. But maybe it was then that I first began to understand and appreciate the element of choice in our situation, which set us apart from our neighbours.

I chose not to look for a job when I left teacher training college. At the time, I had no aspirations to be a teacher at all. I was content to be at home, to give myself time and space to adjust to married life, a new home, and to make new friends.

Stephen had plenty of pressure from his job, and it didn't seem the least bit desirable for me to place myself under similar pressure too, although there were, at that time, enough jobs available had I wanted one.

As ever, subtle forces were at work. There were those among our friends and family who thought it irresponsible or unwise of me not to work. There were those who thought (wrongly) that it was Stephen's decision that I shouldn't work. And, after a year or so, there were those who made discreet enquiries as to our fertility: if I wasn't working, they concluded, surely I must be trying to start a family?

I wasn't always very good at resisting those pressures, and even had occasional half-hearted bursts of job-hunting. (I was once employed by the DHSS for a fortnight, as an envelope-addresser. It was required that I sign the Official Secrets Act, so I read every last punctuation mark first, just in case there were any hidden clauses for envelope-addressers. There weren't.)

Broodiness finally set in, so we bought our house. We sensed dismay among some members of my family, who had, ironically, been brought up in the very same district some half a century earlier. They found it painfully hard to accept or understand the changes that had taken place.

Nevertheless, we stuck to our decision to stay. A year later, Thomas was born at four-thirty on a Sunday morning. Stephen, by then a trainee lay reader, finally staggered from

7

the hospital after an exhausting and exhilarating night, to preach at the morning service.

Two and a half years later, we repeated the exercise. Alexis was born at four-thirty on a Sunday morning, and Stephen (by now well-practised) staggered off to deliver his sermon.

We haven't gone for a hat-trick. Our sons were planned babies and we were able to wait until we could buy a house before having a family. All along it was our choices that decided our lives.

But I can think of so many people in Toxteth who have never had these 'choices' in the way I have. One is Soraya, who must have been about eight years old when we first moved into our house. She lived close by with her mother, a flamboyant West Indian. I first noticed Soraya in the act of removing a bottle of milk from another neighbour's doorstep. Both Stephen and I were interested by this discovery – we had often wondered why we found ourselves a pint short in the mornings. Nowadays we buy milk from the supermarket. The amount you pay for and the amount you put in the fridge corresponds that way.

Ten years later Soraya has two children. The older one is at school. Soraya is now a handsome, intelligent girl and still lives with her mum. She looks much older than eighteen. She suffers from depression, severe enough for spells in hospital.

I recently read an article in a woman's magazine about four women in their late thirties, and the varied choices they made for their lives. All had had highly successful careers in business. Two had chosen not to have children, one was a working mother. The fourth had decided to give up her career and concentrate on full-time parenting and homemaking. She had three pre-school children, and was utterly content.

She is old enough to be Soraya's mother. She has a life-time of experiences, of working and travelling, of developing

8

interests and hobbies, of buying and furnishing a home and cultivating a garden.

All those women were free to make their choices. Soraya has, I suppose, made hers too. By the time she's in *her* late thirties, she'll probably be a grandmother. Will she have a husband? A job? Her own home? The custody of her children?

Stories like Soraya's can be multiplied, many, many times, the world over. Only, here it seems to happen again and again, in one way or another. Why, in these days of readily available contraception, of the apparent freedom of 'a woman's right to choose', of supposed sexual equality, of sex education, do so many girls still become mothers so young?

There can be no easy answers. But imagine for a moment that you are a young woman with no future, no status, no prospects. Start pushing a pram along the street, and suddenly you have all three: the baby is your future, you have status as a mother, you have the prospect of somewhere of your own to live. Of course, it's not that simple. But when life offers, or seems to offer, infinite varieties of nothing, having a baby may appear an attractive alternative.

Maggie is a friend who lives a few streets away from us. I first got to know her when we gave birth to our first children within days of each other. As I write this, she is pregnant with her fourth child. She's younger than me, but looks ten years older. Her clothes are functional, her appearance careworn.

I wonder how similar our expectations were when she gave birth to Darren and I gave birth to Thomas? There was one obvious difference which didn't reflect so much on us ourselves: Stephen was as involved in the process of the birth as the hospital staff allowed, while it was Maggie's mother who supported her through her labour (and her subsequent ones).

Maggie knew that it would be she who would shoulder the

9

responsibilities of child-rearing, which now include a cleaning job to supplement her income. She knew, too, that any family planning would be her responsibility.

Her three sons are well-mannered, quiet children, and Maggie has much to be proud of in them. But the cost, for her, has been her youth and vitality. Not yet thirty, it seems that the next milestone she has to look forward to is becoming a grandmother.

And how very many others is that also true of: old-young women, translated from children into housewives overnight? And for what? To nurture a new generation of child-mothers, unemployed fathers, dreams dissolving into disillusionment, and disillusionment into despair.

I'm unimpressed by the arguments that everyone has an equal chance in this country, and that, if you're motivated enough, you can succeed. It amounts to no more than telling someone to pull him/herself up by the bootstraps. Life and its opportunities *may* all be up for grabs, but if you're near the bottom of the pile to begin with, you can be sure that all the best bits will have gone by the time you fight your way to the top, if you have the nature of a fighter in you. And the most you can probably hope for is scraps and other people's rejects.

I've known Sharon on and off for several years. Her older children are at school with my boys, and we often chat at the school gates, her baby bouncing in his pram, and her three year old, a veteran two-wheeler cyclist, racing round the playground as we wait for the school bell.

Sharon has, I reckon, as much cause for complaint as anyone I know. Her husband spends much of his life detained at Her Majesty's pleasure, reappearing periodically. Nine months or so later his child is born, but he has long since vanished again.

With four small children, Sharon's time is fully occupied. She wouldn't be able to fit in a paid job, should there be any chance of finding one.

Hers is a pretty tough life, yet I always feel cheered when I see her. Invariably she's grinning, and greets her children with hugs and jokes. Some say she shouldn't let her husband use her like that. Yet she has an unusual courage, choosing to face her options single-handed, managing to make the best of her circumstances.

Janet has a hard time too. Four children, like Sharon; and a husband with a drink problem and poor health. Somehow, though, she doesn't come through it all like Sharon. Her children are taken into care from time to time. She and her husband take it in turns to leave each other, but somehow they all end up together again.

Her money frequently runs out before the end of the week, and we're often called on to bail them out. Her daughter arrives on our doorstep with a note, requesting a loaf of bread and some tea-bags and a pint of milk.

The eldest boy has got involved with a gang of young thieves (although he's barely older than Thomas). More than once Janet has said to me, 'I don't think I can go on. I can't take any more of this,' indicating by her gesture the squabbling children, the mess of the home.

Why does one person appear to come out on top, and one go under? Janet's needs are mostly obvious; yet the deepest needs aren't being met, or surely she would be able to cope as Sharon does.

And yet, Sharon has many needs too. By the standards of this country she lives well below the poverty line. She experiences abuse and neglect from her husband. Her children are still too young to appreciate the implications of their father's lengthy absences.

Because Janet shouts loudly, help is soon at hand. But it only serves to alleviate the pain temporarily. And because Sharon doesn't shout at all, it seems to everyone that all is well. Thank God for her sunny, uncomplaining disposition. I pray that no one takes advantage of it.

In this rights-conscious generation, many people in inner-city areas like ours feel genuine grievances at the infringement of what are held to be their rights. What about the right to work, and to a realistic wage or a decent Social Security payment? The right to adequate housing, effective education, reasonable local amenities? The right to be free of racial harassment, of sexual harassment, of police harassment, or of local government ineptitude? Many rights, many freedoms.

None of these issues should be too readily dismissed. We may have an immediate reaction to them born out of our own experience, but we must learn to listen, to stand in the other person's shoes, to *want* to understand.

When did you, if you are a white person, last experience racial abuse? When were you, if a man, last compromised sexually? When did you, if an employer, last waste whole mornings in dole queues?

The rights of the defenceless and oppressed need to be defended by our awareness, and our consequent prayer and action. Many books have been written to address such issues. The evidence is all there. God *is* on the side of the poor and the oppressed. Whatever else Jesus was talking about in the parable of the sheep and the goats (Matthew 25. 31–46), the base line is charity. Am I to refuse a cup of water to a communist? Does an AIDS sufferer forfeit my care? God forbid.

Our hearts need to be in touch with God's heart, hurting where he hurts, loving whom he loves. Unless he leads me to be a full-time high-profile campaign worker, it's unlikely that I can do more than scratch at a surface or two of the needs that I am aware of. But as I follow where he leads, as I listen to his voice, then, if I am willing, I may find myself involved in redressing the balance of inequality, showing solidarity with another person; maybe letting God turn my prejudices inside out.

What about personal decisions I make about *my* own life,

home, career, and so on? Surely I must choose what is best for myself and my family, so far as I am able? Just as long as I remain aware that, for every one person who can exercise these basic freedoms in the world today, approximately four cannot. As long as I am aware that, in the scores of neglected urban communities of our nation, the majority of citizens cannot. As long as I believe that, for each of these others, the rights that I assume as being unquestionably, naturally mine, should also be unquestionably, naturally theirs also. That is the moral tension I need to hold in balance when I exercise the power of choice in my, or my family's life.

No one should have to feel guilty about how much they possess. Good things are a gift from God, whether they are to be found in the natural world, or have been made. We need loveliness in our lives, we need fun, we need the joy of giving and receiving gifts. It is good to have exotic meals occasionally, to celebrate with friends, to benefit from exciting or relaxing holidays. What hurts is that not everyone can experience these things. Even the natural environment for some is ravaged, or is ravaging.

That is why our values, if we are Christians, are turned upsidedown (or Godsideup). If we don't understand sorrow, we cannot fully understand joy. If we haven't known imprisonment, we cannot fully appreciate freedom.

Some years ago, I came across a small out-of-print book, written by a missionary in China. Its very title challenged me so much that I didn't dare open it for a long time – *Have we no right?* Eventually I gritted my teeth and started to read. In the first chapter, the author writes of a time she found herself listening to the words of an older missionary.

'You know', he began, 'there's a great deal of difference between *eating bitterness* (Chinese idiom for suffering hardship) and *eating loss* (Chinese idiom for suffering the infringement of one's rights).

'Eating bitterness' is easy enough. To go out with the preaching band, walk twenty or thirty miles to the place where you are to work, help set up the tent . . . and spend several weeks in a strenuous campaign of meetings and visitation. Why, that's a thrill!

'Your beds may be made of a couple of planks laid on sawdust, and you may have to eat boiled rice, greens and bean-curd three times a day . . . but it's good for anyone to go back to the simple life! A little healthy "bitterness" is good for anybody! That hasn't troubled me particularly . . . *Another thing* that I had never thought about came up to make trouble. I had to "eat loss"! I found that I couldn't stand up for my rights – that I couldn't even *have* any rights. I found that I had to give them up, every one, and that was the hardest thing of all.'

This author soon discovered for herself what it meant to 'eat loss'. Missionaries, she explained, are programmed to expect to 'eat bitterness'. There's even an element of romance and excitement there.

'Eating loss', the giving up of one's rights, or of having one's own way, is what Jesus did when he 'denied himself'. And so the missionary turned the challenge back to the reader: 'What rights must be given up that a Christian at home would not have to give up?'

Dare I face that question, and address it to myself; and then be ready to listen to the answer?

3

Broken Glass and Graffiti

I have created a mind-picture of the kind of environment I want to bring my children up in, if such a choice were given to me. It's not unreasonable or impossible. Many assume it as their right.

There is a spacious house. Largish, oldish, with big rooms. There are gardens with trees, vegetables and flower borders. Plenty of grass, though not necessarily wall-to-wall carpeted lawns. Birds, nests, various animals (though large Alsatians don't feature). There's water: pond, lake, stream, river – any or all. Parkland, fields, more trees – woodland, forest. Then hills. Space. Fresh air and space.

There's a saying that the grass on the other side is always greener. That's invariably true as far as I'm concerned: there isn't any grass where I live. (Plenty of Alsatians to spare, though.)

I want to give my sons space – physical space – in a pleasant environment. I want rooms big enough for them to roll and jump around in. Nine year olds need a *lot* of space. Space for the club they want to form. Space to shout in. Space to creep away and be secret and quiet in, to have a private sulk or a weep in. Space enough in the kitchen so that they can comfortably bake or cook alongside me. (Lord, remind me of that one if ever I *do* happen to have a kitchen big enough.)

And a garden. You've got to have one or the other, space inside or out, preferably both. Children are like pressure cookers, forever having to let off steam, loudly, energetically and fast.

We don't have those things. We have a small terraced

15

house with small rooms and a tiny yard cut in half by a bathroom extension.

I want a garden for my sons to play in and appreciate. I want to be able to give them a bit of soil to cultivate. I may conveniently forget that I frequently neglected the plot of earth that was my very own in my father's garden, but at least I had that choice, to dig it or walk past it. And then that was probably because greater adventure lay on the other side of the hedge, in the farmland beyond.

We do have a garden – one foot by five feet, plus two chimney pots and a porcelain kitchen sink. Unfortunately our front garden (a hanging basket) fell off the wall last year. Over our back wall is an alley, or entry, strewn with the entrails of dog-savaged bin bags and the occasional (live) rat. I think that the appeal its forbiddenness has for the boys is outweighed by their natural distaste for it.

Happily, they can play in the street. Balls and bikes are sometimes stolen, sometimes retrieved. There is bullying and cruelty of the childish kind, but they cope. Children, they say, are great survivors. But street play is limited and limiting. There's no privacy. Bikes, balls and so on become communal. You can't erect a tent or dig a hole (at least, not without a great deal of effort), or have a picnic or make a den. As a parent, a part of you is always on guard, against accident (the road ours leads on to witnesses the most erratic driving I've ever seen off the TV screen), against fights and bullying and the tensions that occasionally flare up in the area.

There is a park, but I wouldn't allow my children there unaccompanied. So as far as any practical freedom of access goes on a daily basis, it might as well be miles away.

What does any parent want for his or her child? I would suggest health and wholeness – hopefully physical health, but if not that, certainly emotional and (if they are aware of that dimension) spiritual wholeness. And probably material prosperity. Certainly happiness. Oscar Wilde said, 'The

16

best way to make children good is to make them happy.'

Yet we can guarantee none of it. We have to hold our children in an open palm, although we long to hold them tight to us, to protect them from dangers or chance things which may blow or snatch them away. But if we hold them tight to us, they will be crushed and suffocated.

Despite the risks and the certainty of some degree of failure, I long to give my children the best that I can. The best start to life, good opportunities, security, exposure to God's love. Imperfectly, we can give them these things. As we ourselves are loved by God, by each other, and by ourselves, so our measure of love available for them increases.

I went through a phase of guilt when the boys were small, worrying about the time – or the quality of the time – I spent with them, forever hearing of how quickly they grow up.

I tied myself in knots trying to be a creative mother, constantly providing them with stimulation of a 'useful' kind, while simultaneously aiming to achieve perfection in the roles of wife, lover, woman, friend . . . a familiar story. All these marvellous pictures on the kitchen wall created from pasta shells and lentils – who benefits more, I wonder: the child (who executed the masterpiece in about five minutes flat), or the mother (who also spent the next half hour cleaning the bits off the table, the walls, the floor and the child)? I remember that, as a child, my great joy was to play with my mother's button box, though I wonder now if the happy hours so spent were in fact happy five or ten minutes, plus a further bad-tempered ten or more putting them away.

I fell into the trap of comparing myself with other women I looked up to, and invariably failed to match up. Now, I know that they too sometimes shut the front door, and scream at their children, at their husbands (if they have one), at the world, at God . . .

One day I tried to remember what had meant most to me about my mother (who died when I was sixteen) when I was a child. The general sense I had was of being loved, of feeling secure. There were images of her being around somewhere, but not necessarily right where I was. She was there when I needed her, and that made me feel secure. Her love was conveyed to me time and again, in cuddles and romps, in secret minutes together, in story-telling, at bedtime. So I didn't mind her being busy because I knew that none the less I was central to her affections. Her priorities could alter, should I be frightened, or ill, or just needing someone to notice me.

I can aim to give this to my sons, I realise, equally well in the heart of Toxteth as in any rural or suburban setting. So *why* do I still hanker for a different physical environment? The reasons are subtle and sometimes contradictory.

Parents want what they see as the best for their children. Sometimes it's because they experienced some degree of deprivation or thwarted ambition when they were growing up themselves. I feel guilty when I think of things I enjoyed as a child (a garden, for example) which I am denying my sons. Adults may choose to deny themselves certain privileges, but is it fair on their children?

And what of advertising? However much we may deny its influence, the insidious pressures at work on all sides can conspire to make anyone feel inadequate, or at least dissatisfied with their circumstances.

There's a further danger for Christians, in the message of material blessing being a sign of God's favour. I think that Christians spend far more time justifying their material benefits than they would their poverty. When we lack such benefits, when we find ourselves jobless, or in debt, or without a car or washing machine, *is* it because we haven't tithed faithfully, or haven't thanked and praised and believed for them enough?

In all of this, of course, there can be truth. But material blessing of itself is neither good nor bad; rather, it is our attitude towards it that is its moral dimension. That includes Toxteth dwellers and stockbroker-belt dwellers alike. We don't have to possess riches to have an attitude towards them. I can be bitter and cynical and poor. I can be bitter and cynical and rich.

There are testimonies without number of God's provision for the needs of his people, from the book of Genesis through to the 1980s. But to those Christians who live in prosperous residential areas with high employment, the perspective differs from that of Christian inhabitants of decaying inner cities with high unemployment.

So what *do* I want for my children? Hearts hungry for God, hearts open to love his world in all its awesome majesty and brute ugliness, hearts to love all his creatures, joyful and glorious, bruised and broken.

I had the opportunity to grow up in a visually lovely environment. My sons have the opportunity to grow up in a multi-ethnic, multi-cultural one. I learnt of the work of missionaries in the 'dark continents'; they hurt when their friends are the butt of racist attacks. I learnt the names of wild flowers and played on river banks; they wonder at the incredible rate of growth of the ferns in the back-yard chimney pots each spring, and at the sun setting over the Mersey at Pier Head. I talked to geese through the hedge in the garden; Alexis stroked and crooned to a dead rat in the corner of a concreted play area (until his father discovered the object of his affections).

When the 'injustice' of it all overwhelms me, I pour it all out to my Father God (and to one or two longsuffering friends), just as I encourage the boys to tell us about the things that hurt and/or upset them, that seen unfair or unreasonable.

Find rest, O my soul, in God alone;
my hope comes from him.

He alone is my rock and my salvation:
he is my fortress, I shall not be shaken.
My salvation and my honour depend on God;
he is my mighty rock, my refuge.
Trust in him at all times
. . . pour out your hearts to him.

(Psalm 62.5–8)

4

'Suffer Little Children . . . '

I suppose that most parents want to protect their children, to foster their sense of the essential goodness of things, and to preserve their innocence a little longer. It was a good story to tell our friends, the one about Alexis and his dead rat. But when I think about it in the night sometimes, it makes my heart ache because it seems to encapsulate the stained and broken quality of inner-city living. It only becomes bearable for me because I know that God listens, cares and understands too.

There's so much I want to protect my sons from; from abuse of language to abuse of animals, from the mistreatment of property to the mistreatment of people.

Will what they see and hear make them wiser and more compassionate, or will it dull their sensitivity? Will they become more aggressive or, perhaps, more anxious and withdrawn than they would have done in a less damaged atmosphere? Shouldn't *I* shelter them from the uglier events, or should I consider more deeply what it means to let them 'stand on their own two feet'?

When newsworthy events have occurred in Granby over the years (such as arson attacks on cars or buildings, car chases, or police raids), Stephen and I choose to avoid the scene or remain inside, rather than turn it into a spectator event, as many do, especially children and teenagers.

The boys have often been with us when prostitutes were being solicited. So far they have been able to put a quite innocent interpretation on the scene, in so far as they were aware of it. While this is so, we feel no need to enlighten them.

A young friend who lives nearby didn't have any such choice. For Phil, prostitution was as ordinary as bread and jam. His mum used to take him with her down to the docks to visit the sailors; prostitution was her trade.

When he reached school age, he was taken into care, and fostered by a loving family, where he has been for some years now. At first glance, he seems to be a happy, energetic, well-adjusted lad. As I got to know him better, I discovered underneath a far less secure child, who makes lots of superficial relationships but has no close friends. Indeed, when friendships start to deepen, he drops those friends and moves on to others.

What fruit will be produced from those early years down at the docks? What concepts are already formed in Phil's mind about love and friendship, sexual relationships and parenthood? And what of his natural mother? How does she cope with the experience of having lost her child, albeit through her own inadequacy and neglect?

The subject of abortion was raised at our dinner table recently. 'What if a mother is pregnant but doesn't want to have the baby? Can she stop it being born?' Thomas asked. Not a subject I would have chosen to debate with the boys anywhere at this stage, and not one that rates highly on my list of meal-time topics of conversation. So I simply said that yes, sometimes women do stop their babies from being born. Such a notion stunned the boys, and out tumbled questions about what happened to the babies, and did they go to heaven, and would they grow up there. So we digressed naturally from the issue of abortion itself, and I didn't choose to raise it again just then.

I wish, oh how I wish, that I could tell my children that the world is wonderful and happy and harmonious, full stop. It *is* those things, we *do* rejoice in the wonder and beauty of creation and of the achievements of the human race. But Thomas and Alexis know already that all is not as it should be. We often talk about racism. We've discussed divorce and one-parent families. They're aware that some of their friends have brothers and sisters with different fathers. They've confronted atheism and blasphemy, and have some understanding of the conflicts within the Christian Church, as well as between other religions. They know that some of their friends mistrust the police.

We try (and try and try again) to maintain a harmony within our home, consciously acknowledging Jesus to be head of the home. And every time we blow it, we say sorry to him, and to each other, and start again. We do a lot of starting again in our house.

I find it hard to judge how the boys are affected by living in Toxteth. They seem pretty normal kids to me. Nevertheless, excepting those who have felt God's call to do so, or some with a strong (generally left-wing) political ideology, I'm not sure I know anyone who would *choose* to bring up their children here. Some who live outside the area – and it's only a short bus ride to a quite different environment – think we are wrong to continue to live here. No one in our families is really happy about our being here, particularly with the boys in mind. Of the many mothers I've chatted with over the last year or so, nearly all would move out of the area if the opportunity arose. For the majority, it won't.

What kind of things do Stephen and I feel at odds with here? There's the language of course. Not Scouse, but Language – with a capital L. There is a constant exposure to swearing and blasphemy for the boys, as much from their contemporaries as anyone else. How this affects their own vocabulary, and so their thought patterns, I'm not sure. I'm most impressed by their chameleon ability to change their speech-register in mid-sentence if necessary, becoming completely Scouse to greet a passing friend.

But swearing is, of itself, the least of my concerns. The underlying attitude of so many people here seems to be aggressive in one way or another, of which swearing and blasphemy are often first symptoms. To see small (I mean three and four year old) children shouting 'Pigs' after policemen is disturbing. Nor is it pleasant to be on the receiving end of verbal abuse oneself from children as I have, for a variety of reasons, from time to time. Such anger and aggression is learnt at home, sometimes consciously taught. It's a survival technique. You've got to be hard to survive.

Frankie and Andrea are two very different people who have toughened up to get by around here.

No one had to teach me how to love Thomas and Alexis, and no one had to teach them how to respond to that love. It all came naturally. Frankie, on the other hand, hasn't had much opportunity to find out if love comes naturally or not. He's a little older than Thomas, and lives in the next street. He started to attend an after-school club, but after only a couple of weeks, he stopped going. His mates said it was because Alf, one of the club workers, had been picking on him. That simply wasn't like Alf. He'd just tried to show Frankie a better way of doing an activity he was learning.

Though Frankie looks tough on the outside, it doesn't go very deep. His mother rejected him when he was a baby, and he had been brought up by another woman in the street, who had several children of her own, all of whom had different fathers.

So Frankie saw Alf's concern to correct and teach him not only as a criticism of his ability in a particular area, but as a rejection of his very self. And so he reacted by bold, bluff denouncing of the club with its leaders and members as generally worthless – not something he wanted to be involved in anyway.

Where will he end up? School has no appeal; nor has church any more. The rough exterior will gradually harden into an armour-plated defence which he will learn to rely on more and more, so that anyone who comes up against it will probably get hurt. After all, a reputation for being hard is likely to keep you safe. He will probably treat women badly; but then, he will only be drawing on his past experiences to guide him.

Frankie is white. At least he doesn't have to fight against racism too (against himself, that is). Andrea, whom I first met at a mother and toddlers group, is black, and you don't have to live very long in a mixed-race community to discover that racism, in one form or another, has wormed its way into every corner of society, churches included.

By nature gentle, Andrea has consciously adopted an assertive (some may say aggressive) stance, in order to appear self-confident and assured. She states loudly and clearly that black is beautiful. It's not so hard to understand why, when round and about, vicious slogans are painted large across walls by the National Front and the ANS (Anti-Nigger Squad).

Andrea is married to a fair-haired white man. So their daughters look, at first glance, like white children.

Some years ago, Andrea told me that she intended to bring up her daughters to look on themselves as fundamentally black children. I couldn't understand it at the time. It seemed to me at best petty and illogical; at worst, a form of inverted racism.

Now I do understand a little. We don't have to struggle if we're white in the UK. Being white makes you part of the majority, part of the status quo. No one queries *our* origins because of the colour of our skin. No one has a prejudicial attitude towards us because we're born white; there's no sense of shame, of inferiority, of worthlessness, of being different because we're white.

Andrea recognises that Shirley and Leanne will be assumed to be white without anyone giving it a second thought. There'll be no struggle, no need to prove their worth as citizens of the UK because of their colour. It would be easy to forget their heritage – their African ancestry, and the richness of that continent which is theirs to rejoice in as well as their European heritage.

They need to be *proud* to have both a black mother and a white father. They should be able to delight in the possibility that their babies could be black or white. Andrea's daughters should be free to grow up with a sense of being doubly blessed, not of being racially handicapped. And yet they will be treated as such by so many. The fact that many local blacks are British by several generations still doesn't count in the eyes of people who apparently believe – so their attitudes tell us – that the real person, the soul and spirit of a person, is only skin deep.

Aggression is something I've never coped with well. I'm pretty sure that I lost the few childhood fights that I was involved in as much from cowardice as anything more altruistic. The fact is, I still don't have an answer to the dilemma faced by many parents, of how to teach your children to deal with aggression. I recall occasions when my sons were being thumped by small contemporaries. (They did their fair share of thumping too.) Their friends' parents encouraged mine to retaliate, 'Go on, hit him back! Go on, batter him!' Thomas and Alexis were, as it happened, generally disinclined to do so.

On more than one occasion I've seen mothers come to physical blows as the result of their offspring's fisticuffs. And having experienced the overwhelming emotions in myself that surface after another's attack (verbal or physical) on my children, I can understand the passions that spark off such brawls.

Some time ago, an angry mother bawled out at the kids, including one of mine, playing in the street for apparently victimising her (considerably older) son. Whatever the rights or wrongs concerned, she would have done better to leave well alone. The result was a furious retaliation from another mother, and a vindictive and offensive exchange of insults ensued. As ever, the mothers' bitterness festers, and the children are caught in between.

All children fight, physically or verbally, playfully or aggressively. Their grievances may be genuine, their frustrations manifold. Round here, boys are still, by and large, expected to be tough and macho. This is reflected in their games, and in their toys. Against this backcloth and soundtrack, how do you teach a boy that to be gentle isn't to be soft, that to be strong isn't of necessity to be a tough fighter? When do I turn a blind eye, and when do I intervene? How do I channel aggression in an environment that breeds and often actively encourages it?

When Thomas has been unduly provoked in the playground and responded by throwing punches, I don't generally consider it appropriate to remind him of Jesus' words in Matthew 5.39: 'If someone strikes you on the right cheek, turn to him the other also.' Even less so, if he has hit out (as happens) on behalf of someone else who has been subjected to bullying. A more useful focus and encouragement for him would be Matthew 5.9: 'Blessed are the peacemakers, for they will be called sons of God.'

Anne Townsend's book *Families Without Pretending* approaches family life as most of us actually experience it, which is very comforting. She describes the dichotomy many parents experience between how the 'pseudo-psychologists' who write in popular magazines think our children should be allowed to 'express' their feelings (especially those of aggression) in order to grow up without hang-ups, and the form that such expression might take. 'I cannot believe', she writes, 'that I am to interpret this to mean that I can allow . . . my children to throw custard pies in the faces of those adults whom they dislike.'

Children do need to express the multitude of emotions that they experience. How does a Christian parent teach children

27

to love their enemies and pray for their persecutors, as Jesus instructs, when they are brimful of righteous anger and vengeful wrath?

I'm left with another question too: What do you do when existing social conventions may allow for *adults* to throw custard pies – or worse – at each other?

If children learn by the example of their elders, I wonder what lesson was learnt by the small child I observed in Granby Street a few years ago, as he was beaten about by a man with a stick, with several other adults standing around at a safe distance, not interfering. I too remained at a safe distance, my excuse being that I had a two year old with me and didn't want him to see.

Television poses a problem or two, ones I know can be universally experienced. We face, however, a double dichotomy: our standards are different from those of many others primarily because we're Christians, but also because our values are often socio-culturally at variance with those held locally. The two aspects overlap and get confused: am I offended at this because I'm a Christian, or because of my aesthetic or cultural sensibilities? Do I approve of that because it is primarily spiritually uplifting, or because it reinforces my set of social values?

Observation leads me to assume that in most local households, the TV is switched on at breakfast, and remains on until the last person goes to bed. Children's bedtimes appear to be very flexible, so that the protection against their viewing unsuitable material, afforded by the 9.00 p.m. 'adult programme' watershed employed by the television companies is rendered ineffective. In fact, the bed of one young child my husband taught was blankets, quite literally under the television set.

Just now a neighbour called round, asking advice. The problem: two small boys in the next street have been seen torturing and mutilating pigeons. The same boys stand on the walls at the back of the houses further up our street and urinate into the yards. Their mother, I'm told, slams the door in the face of anyone who has called to make a complaint. Shocking? Christians, at least, can't afford to be shocked by human nature. Unusual? Not really. Another neighbour's dog – a gentle, loveable animal – bears scars resulting from a spate of knife attacks from local children. Fewer than half of the vigorous new trees planted locally can expect to survive the destructive attention paid to them. A glass milk or pop bottle becomes a toy (and, very occasionally, ammunition). It provides a few moments of fun – maybe through a window, more usually smashed on the pavement or road, and may subsequently provide hours of frustration or misery for its victims. Yesterday I followed the very bloodly trail of a dog which had unwittingly encountered a broken bottle.

Jesus said we must let little children come to him. He went further, instructing us to become like little children ourselves. The winsome, bright-eyed innocents we probably imagine contrast strangely with these tough, street-wise kids. Which do you picture sitting on Jesus' knee?

I am always moved by the account in Luke Chapter 7 of Jesus dining with a Pharisee, when he was anointed with perfume by a prostitute. The intimacy, the tenderness, the compassion, the prophetic insight . . . All have power to touch the reader's heart.

One particular time, however, I realised with a shock that I always pictured the woman as being very beautiful, young, shapely. Now as I looked again, I saw a hard-faced street-woman, body stretched and thickened with age, hair lank and matted, skin sallow and pitted. The romantic aura faded, but the depth of the compassion of God in my mind-picture was greatly magnified.

I guess I easily imagine Thomas and Alexis perched happily on Jesus' knee. I can imagine the desolate and bewildered children of the Boat People there too. And the famine victims of Africa. But what of the lads who maliciously bullied Alexis in front of me? What of the thirteen year olds who exposed themselves to me at the top of the street? What of the lads who kicked our front door in for fun? Maybe they need to be *over* someone's knee from time to time. But do they not also need to be embraced by the loving arms of Jesus, as their father, mother, big brother, best mate . . . ?

It's easy to love our 'nice' neighbours, the ones who share our values, our standards, our life-style. There's a mutual reinforcement of the 'rightness' of our way of life, a comfortableness about it all.

But it's becoming increasingly hard to put across to children the fundamental Christian principle of loving your neighbour (let alone your enemy). They now get taught (of cruel necessity) to be wary of friendly adults, to be careful when playing with older children. 'Stranger: Danger' rhymes are recited alongside the traditional ones.

Children get on with being nice to each other just as long as the mood is reciprocated. They bristle and retaliate and harbour grudges over the slightest provocation. (As do most grown-ups, only we've learnt how to cover up better.) Our boys have had ample opportunity to learn about the cost as well as the theory of forgiveness. Of course, it may be singularly inappropriate to approach a large bully and offer conciliation. He just may not appreciate it.

Our boys don't always want to forgive straight away, as is the case for me too, when they've been wronged. They need space to cool down, and in their own time they're ready. Ordering them to say sorry at once, demanding that they forgive *now*, doesn't allow time for a necessary attitude of repentance and a genuine desire for reconciliation.

I wonder at the build-up of resentment and unforgiveness in many of the homes around us. Hardly a day passes that I don't overhear a snippet of conversation, one relating to the other the faults of a third party, and how the aggrieved intends to be avenged. The two mothers who rowed over their respective children simply refuse to speak to each other. And so the children learn how to behave. Some are actively encouraged *not* to forgive. Saying sorry is weak. 'I shan't forget what you did,' is a measure some people employ, and it can be as good as a curse in its effects, both on the offended and the offender.

It may all seem rather grim, raising kids in Toxteth. As ever, the good things get taken for granted, and we forget to be thankful for them.

In his book *If I Were Starting My Family Again*, John Drescher writes, 'I see now that I was, many times, much too serious. While my children loved to laugh, I, too often, must have conveyed the idea that being a parent was very painful and a perennial problem.' Maybe it is, but that's a problem to be *dealt* with.

'Sons are a heritage from the Lord, children a reward from him' (Psalm 127.3). If they would wear them, I ought to embroider that verse on headbands so that I would read it every time I looked at my sons. There are times when I act as if these little ones were a punishment rather than a reward, as if they were a mistake, and not longed-for, planned and precious.

God, forgive me. And have mercy on all the other fathers and mothers who seem to twist that eternal truth into a cruel jest in their reactions and attitudes.

5

Veil of Fear

'How did your weekend go?' I asked Lin. She and Jeff had just come back from what amounted to a second honeymoon, a weekend in Herefordshire, with the children happily installed back home with friends and family. 'It was wonderful. But we couldn't get over how nice everyone was – living around here, you forget how friendly people and places can be.'

We laughed and talked of other things. But I thought about it afterwards. One of the kicks, you could call it, that I get when we go to Devon for our summer holiday, is to be among openly friendly fellow humans. Not necessarily soul-baring, tell-it-all types, simply people who automatically exchange a greeting or pass the time of day with you; or just meet your eye without instinctively averting their glance. An almost guaranteed friendly reception at the supermarket check-out; freedom to take a stroll on a starry evening.

Nowhere, of course, can it be like that all of the time. Sometimes we're so engrossed in our own thoughts that we simply don't notice anyone else. We all have 'off' days, and choose not to acknowledge the rest of the world. The check-out girl runs out of merry quips on a Friday afternoon. And muggers and rapists don't lurk exclusively in inner-city streets and alleys.

If you've been out today, you've probably greeted several people and hardly noticed that it happened. Invariably I'm conscious of when I've greeted someone, because it's no longer an automatic response. The first – automatic – response on approaching a stranger tends to be one of suspicion. 'I'm unsure of your intentions as you approach . . . I may even feel afraid. Do you feel contempt towards me because I'm white? Are you about to make a sexually suggestive remark? Do you have designs on my purse?' I guess if I was to analyse my split-second reaction on the approach of some strangers, one of these thoughts may flit across my mind.

Happily, a smile works wonders. Assuming you can catch someone's eye – many automatically avoid looking at someone else – after the initial uncertainty, it's like the sun coming out. It seems like a lot of fuss about nothing. But it is yet another factor in the process of alienation, of estrangement, of the fragmentation of this society. I guess it's a fairly common experience in inner cities everywhere, the world over.

Is there any foundation for my feelings, any evidence to justify the caution and suspicion so many exercise round here? Or is it simply fear breeding fear? I've never experienced any real personal threat here – occasional verbal abuse or intimidation, yes, and at one time, the experience of being solicited by kerb-crawlers was a daily nuisance. That last problem has, happily, been effectively erased by vigorous campaigning a few years ago.

A few of my friends have had bags snatched or purses stolen, in broad daylight as well as in the dark. Recently, an elderly member of our church who lives in the vicinity disturbed an intruder, who beat her over the head.

Some friends, Ruth and Annie, were walking home through the local park one evening, engrossed in the business of catching up on several months' news, as Annie had been working abroad. Ruth, who has two small children, is involved in drama and dance, and Annie was on holiday from the drama company she worked with. Ruth's flat (they've since moved) was on the edge of the park, and was reached either by a walk of a few hundred yards along an unlit path

33

running across the park, or a frequently muddy walk along an unsurfaced, pot-holed road with lots of dark driveways . . . not a pleasant couple of options for a journey home in the dark.

Neither of them was in any way prepared for the attack. It was dark, and their assailant came up silently, wearing dark, heavily padded clothing with only his eyes showing. Annie sensed his presence, and turned aside, pretending to tie a shoe lace . . . but he was stronger, and had obviously planned in advance. His objective quickly became apparent; to beat one woman unconscious in order to rape the other. Both were fit and agile, but no real match for the man.

Ruth became dimly aware of a light on in her flat in the distance, and began to shout out for Tom, her husband, who was at home awaiting their return. The shouting, combined with what defence they could muster, convinced the attacker that it was not worth his while to carry on. Happily, although bruised and battered, neither woman suffered serious physical injury, and they were able to hail a taxi, and travel to the local police station. Happily also, the driver refused payment, and the police were kind and sympathetic.

Christians, as Annie and Ruth are, are no more immune to these kind of attacks than anyone else.

Etched on my memory is a nightmarish incident which happened a few years ago. Living opposite us was a lovely Somali woman, Jan, and her four children. The Somali community here are close-knit and spend much time together; groups of Somali men gather on the street corners whenever the weather is clement enough. The women in their traditional dress spend time together, often at that time at classes in the local Methodist Centre, learning sewing, typing, cooking, and keep-fit, while their children romped in the play group.

I was taking the keep-fit class. The passion for exercise was catching on, and I was, so to speak, one step ahead of the rest of the class. It was all fairly gentle stuff, and plenty of fun – it needed to be, with some women encumbered by pregnant bumps, some by flowing ethnic costumes, and some by the ravages of time, such as stiff backs and excess pounds (and stones). We all discovered bits and pieces that bent and moved, and ached, that we'd forgotten belonged to us.

Jan came to the class, and we became friendly. At first I found it hard to believe that she had such a bad time as she made out, I suppose because she had such a gentle, inoffensive manner, and because she had other close women friends who spoke the same language and understood one another's customs.

Her house was the same as ours: three rooms upstairs, and two living rooms and a kitchen downstairs, with a bathroom extension. I found out that she and her children were made to live on the upper floor of the house, to accommodate her husband's girlfriend, with whom he shared the downstairs rooms. Jan cooked for them all.

In time, a court order ruled that Jan's husband and his girlfriend had to leave. But Jan continued to live under a heavy veil of fear. It seems that her family back in Somalia belonged to a rival political party to that of her husband's family, and there was feuding between them. This animosity had erupted into violence. And Jan's husband's loyalties lay not with her, but with his parents and brothers.

I realised just how afraid she was when she delved into the folds of her skirts one day and drew out the hammer that she concealed there and was never parted from. She was so sure that one day her husband would attempt to kill her, as he had threatened. I was appalled, but there really and truly didn't seem to be anything one could do – there was no evidence to show the police (who are very reluctant to become involved in 'domestic' issues), and there didn't seem to be anywhere else that she could go. And she wanted to stay in her home. We offered what we could in terms of friendship and support, and sometimes I prayed with her (like most of her friends, she was Muslim), and she drew comfort from that.

When the attack came, no one heard a thing. As with Annie and Ruth, the attacker – her husband – wore dark clothing, including a balaclava, quite terrifying in the darkness. Jan lay asleep in bed with her four year old daughter. Her husband beat her mercilessly with an iron rod. Miraculously she fought her way into the street and eventually summoned help from a passing vehicle. No one in the street heard her cries because her vocal chords had been damaged in her husband's attempts to strangle her.

The Somali community rallied round and took care of her children while she was in hospital. When I visited her, I only recognised her by the group of friends around her bed – her face had been so badly battered and broken.

Afterwards she went to stay in the local refuge for battered women. Even with bars across her upstairs window she didn't feel safe from her husband, although the shelter staff preserve the anonymity of the women and children who have taken refuge there, and refuse access to anyone unless the woman involved gives her permission otherwise.

In the middle of one night, without warning, she left with the children. Some time later we heard from her. She had gone to London, to stay with distant relatives. She didn't give her address. I don't suppose you will have read about the incident in your paper, because I don't think it got reported. Maybe it didn't seem important enough, merely a domestic incident. As I remember, the husband received a heavy fine for his brutal attack. Jan just faded out of our lives like a passing shadow.

Many people live, day in and day out, enveloped by fear of one kind or another. I see women from time to time with ugly facial bruises and black eyes. Many men who beat their wives or girlfriends are careful to hurt them where it doesn't show. I don't doubt either that there are some men who bear scars and bruises – I have overheard (not by choice) some frighteningly ugly domestic rows, often in effect carried out in public, because doors or windows are open, or one partner is in the yard, or out in the street, possibly locked out. Daytime and night-time, such rows break out.

Two nights ago Thomas came downstairs in tears, having been awoken by a domestic argument raging away somewhere nearby. I understood how he felt, because I feel physically sick whenever I'm awoken that way. We cuddled each other, and prayed, and he went back to sleep, with the light on for comfort.

It's more than just uncomfortable to hear these violent squabbles. It is so distressing to see how frail relationships are, how apparently unable people are to love, to live in harmony, in peace, in an atmosphere of trust and forgiveness. I guess that the release effected by a verbal attack on another must prevent a physical onslaught to some extent, but the proverb 'sticks and stones may break my bones, but words will never hurt me' is a nonsense.

How many adults carry around a burden of inferiority, for example, because they were told as children that they were no good, useless, or not worth the effort spent on them – albeit in jest, in parental frustration, or by an impatient teacher, or an older brother or sister. Maybe it didn't happen often, but it wormed its way into their unconscious and affects their lives to this day. Many of us live with some degree of emotional handicap because of words carelessly spoken.

I think it's the vitriolic nature of so many of the rows I've heard that shocks me. On what foundation was the relationship under attack built? What concept of love do the antagonists have? What provokes the anger, the hatred, the rage? And what kind, or degree, of reconciliation is there that enables them apparently to continue to live together? Husbands (or live-in boyfriends) are often referred to as 'him' by their wives or girlfriends, who in turn are referred to as 'her', often with a hint of derision, or embarrassment, rarely tenderness. What concepts of love have they inherited from their parents and what kind of love will they teach to their own children?

Some people seem to exist within a shroud of fear, from a very young age, in some cases. The other day in the playground, as I came in to collect Alexis, a larger boy (aged about six) was pummelling, pushing over, then attempting to kick the head of a smaller (maybe four year old) boy. It brought tears to my eyes to see the distress of the smaller boy. As I ran over to intervene, a teacher also saw the incident through her window, and banged on it loudly to attract the boys' attention, so the older boy began to saunter off home. The younger boy struggled up sobbing, oblivious to my assistance, wrapped up in his own rage and fear and pain and humiliation. Only a playground fight, they happen everywhere; but some of these children are already so tough, impervious to discipline, and seemingly insensible to the distress of others. Never underestimate fear in children, either because it seems trivial in comparison to adult experience, or because they don't talk about it – they often have no means to express or communicate effectively, or even conceptualise it, so it stays locked away inside.

Just as many little ones experience fear on a daily basis, so do their older brothers and sisters. Sometimes at night I hear the adolescents, out at times I prefer to be asleep, involved in fights and arguments. And there may be one who is afraid, shouting out his or her fear – my blood runs cold at the sound – and perhaps footsteps running down the street, the pursued fleeing from the pursuers.

And then there are the countless single people, maybe widowed, and the elderly. Many fear to open their doors to callers. Having knocked on the doors of elderly people for a variety of reasons over the years, I'm only too aware of the virtual imprisonment some of them exist in, for fear of what might happen to them if they go out alone; others are afraid to leave their homes for fear of a break-in during their absence.

When I'm out, if I find myself approaching an elderly or infirm person from behind, especially if it's a woman, I try to make my approach audible. How often (and I've done it myself) someone hesitates, looks round anxiously at the sound of approaching footsteps, their knuckles whitening as their grip tightens on their bags. I find myself acting instinctively sometimes; I may cross the road, or walk in it, if I feel uncomfortable about someone approaching me. Other times I feel quite at ease to walk through a group of lads loitering on the pavement. But how sad that anyone should live with that sense of mistrust, always being on the edge of wariness – like animals, assuming that another animal is a threat until proved to be peaceful in its intentions.

There have been lighter moments. There is the story of Lal, a little old lady from our church. Widowed, and becoming rather frail, she decided not long ago to move from the large house that had been her home for so long to a smaller, more manageable terraced house.

She moved gradually, popping back to the old house from time to time to collect more bits and pieces, all the while keeping an eye open for her cat, who had disappeared during all the upheaval.

Early one morning, she arrived to find three burly men stealing her copper piping. Casting caution to the wind, she said, 'It's no good telling you to stop, because you'll only come back after I've gone, and finish the job. So, if you want my pipes, you can jolly well work for them.'

They did, too. In the back yard, she had some enormous stone basins full of soil, and she ordered her robbers to put them in their van, which, with great difficulty, they did. Then she hopped in beside them and directed them to her new house. There they completed the task of unloading them into her new back yard. Soon afterwards her cat reappeared, and all ended happily.

And sometimes the informalities of living in this neighbourhood can be a positive boon. One morning, for example, after dropping the boys at school, my attention was caught by a loud rapping on a window. Turning to investigate, I saw an elderly lady, obviously greatly agitated, beckoning me to go over. At her bidding, I went round to the door of her maisonette and let myself in, with some trepidation, wondering what horror might await me. All was quickly revealed: 'For goodness sake, love, get me out of me corsets.' I don't think that the nurse who, minutes earlier, had strapped her patient into them would have approved of my assistance. I think that they were the surgical variety, but I'm not a connoisseur of corsets. It was a veritable struggle to remove them, but we won in the end, and her relief was a joy to behold.

I also remember the day when my neighbour Betty saw a strange young man disappearing up her stairs one summer's afternoon when the front door was open, and how, with many fierce threats, she frog-marched him out again. I don't suppose he returned in a hurry.

But although incidents like that are easy to smile at, sometimes it's not so much of a joke. Very few in this neighbourhood haven't been through some form of attack on property. We've had a few experiences over the years. The only one that I still feel cross about is the theft of my bicycle from our back yard several years ago. I was in the house when it was stolen, in broad daylight. I really was fond of that bike, which had belonged to a school friend's mother, and was a splendid, sturdy, sensible sort of machine (and probably valuable for being elderly). I only hope its new owners appreciated it as much as I did.

I was quite roundly pregnant with Alexis when our proper break-in occurred. Thomas and I were up the road having lunch at a friend's house, before heading to the local mother and toddlers' group. Passing our house on the way there after our lunch, I decided to drop off some bits and pieces. But I couldn't open the front door – the key turned in the lock but the door had been bolted at the top, on the inside.

I knew at once what had happened. Leaving Thomas with my friends, who disappeared back up the street to phone the police, I went, not a little cautiously, to see what could be seen at the back of the house. The back gate was open, but I didn't venture in any further. Instead I hurried up the street to enlist the aid of a student I knew. The poor man was terrified. Nevertheless he bravely entered in through the back door, with me following closely – because after all, any burglar worth his salt would have scarpered at the sound of the key in the lock, if he hadn't already done so.

In fact that is probably what did happen, as there were various 'valuables' left abandoned. They'd been very efficient, obviously professionals, looking for particular things in particular places. So the mess was 'strategic': the contents of my underwear drawer scattered all over the bedroom, and cupboard shelves swept clean, for example. Actually, it at least provided an excuse to do some spring-cleaning, and my underwear drawer invariably looks as though it's been ransacked anyway.

Fortunately we didn't suffer from the traumatic aftereffects of a break-in that many do, especially the feeling of revulsion that results when uninvited strangers have rooted through all one's very personal and private possessions.

When our neighbour Jean was burgled, she found it a very distressing experience. That was hardly surprising, as she had woken in the middle of the night to find the intruder by her bed. Subsequently she suffered from insomnia for many months.

I was impressed by the timing of our first break-in. The burglars had chosen that precise time because the bin men were around, so there were plenty of clanging and smashing noises to cover the sound of our back-door window being broken. And then they must also have observed my disappearance into my friend's house with bib, high chair, and other lunch-time equipment, and concluded that I would be gone for an hour or so.

We've seen potential housebreakers at work. The usual plan runs something like this: a group of two or three lads stand guard at each end of the street, or at the exits to the entries (that does make sense, really . . .). Another lad disappears down the back entry, checking access to the house they may already have targeted, or simply looking out for a likely opportunity. Our suspicions are aroused when we see a group of lads hanging around on the street corner eyeing the street up and down. Sometimes one or two call at a house under some false pretext just to see if anyone's in. There are suspicious phone calls, too, when the caller hangs up immediately the phone is answered.

If any of us householders become aware of such activity in the street, we stand on our doorsteps and observe the suspects. Folded arms and a rolling pin help. Then we look as if we mean business. Of course, on one or two occasions things have moved fast enough for us to have to phone for the police. No one is ever caught. Either the police take an hour or more to arrive (the nearest police stations are a five minute drive away), or the wail of their sirens tends to have a disappearing effect on would-be housebreakers.

One day I came home to find that our back door, which had a glass window, had been smashed in, but our vigilant neighbours had heard, and chased off the intruders. And when our front door was booted in, I think that it was purely – excuse the pun – for kicks. Now we no longer have glass in our doors inviting boots or hammers, and we're generally pretty burglar-proof. Of course, if someone really wanted to get in, no doubt they'd find a way, but I don't suppose it would be worth their while – there's no colour TV, no video, no up-to-date sound system, no computer. Burglars, take note!

Nor do we own a car, but friends who do have from time to time been inconvenienced by the removal of their car radios, smashed windscreens, slashed tyres and, occasionally, the disappearance of the vehicle in the hands of joyriders. All cars have to be parked in the street as there is no garaging. The local curate's car has been vandalised at least nine times in under three years.

I always close the window and lock the door of any car in which I'm a passenger when travelling locally. It has been known for a gang to force open the door and mug the driver and any passengers, usually at traffic lights but, very occasionally, using the highwayman's technique of a hold-up.

Steve and Debbie are close friends of ours whom we first met at church, and who have experienced much that we have; they too chose to set up home in Toxteth after leaving university. They used to live on the fourteenth floor of a block of flats which, although they were barely twenty years old, have recently been demolished. One day they discovered that their car had been stolen from the car park below. The police were contacted and took all the relevant details. Suddenly, from their birds'-eye view, Steve spotted his car tearing around the surrounding neighbourhood. So began a thrilling car chase, with Steve directing police operations over the phone from his vantage point at the window. The car was finally rounded up in the car park where it belonged.

And of course there is a story of the Liverpool corporation bus which was seen trundling along with no one at the wheel. Later an eight year old boy was charged with stealing and unlawfully driving the vehicle.

Tragically, too many joyriders end up with smashed up cars and smashed up kids. That too is another recurring nightmare – only it's a waking one – the sound of car chases, or races, on the circuit provided by the two parallel roads at either end of our street. Not every night, but often enough, the cars or motorbikes can be heard tearing along the roads and screeching and skidding around the corners. The miracle is that more accidents don't happen. But somehow you always anticipate the crash. When one did happen at the end of our road last year, in the middle of the night, my nerve was quite shattered for a while. Yet every morning the dawn breaks, and somehow the perspective shifts again, and I'm comforted in the knowledge that God's compassions never fail, that 'they are new every morning'.

6

Morning in Omar's

Next to Granby Christian Shop, where I help out once a week, is Omar's Store. Like most shops in Granby, business is slow, so on Thursday mornings, when the local curate and I are in the Christian Shop (see Chapter 11), Omar stands in our doorway, keeping an eye on his own, and we talk about just about everything under the sun.

Omar used to live on the Wirral. When I first got to know him, I assumed he was from the Middle East, because of his name, and because his little shop is full of the essential ingredients for the many African and Asian households in the area, as well as stocking Halal meat. It was obvious too that he was Muslim, so my mistake wasn't surprising.

In fact Omar is a Lancashire lad, with a Protestant father and a Catholic mother. But their faith was nominal, and Omar was searching for deeper spiritual reality. He liked what he knew about Jesus, but was left cold by what he witnessed in the so-called Christians round about him, and in their churches.

While at college in Chester, he met some Asian students, and their life-style impressed him. Unlike most groups of young men that he knew, they didn't end up drinking, fighting or womanising each night. They were friendly and good company, and Omar saw a sense of purpose in their lives that he wanted but didn't have.

They were Muslims. Over a period of time, Omar read up all he could about their religion. He thought it would demand too much of him, and almost gave up his study. But then one day, as he put it, 'It simply happened. And when I changed, I felt really relieved, like someone had taken all the weight off me, because we believe that once you change, you're re-born, in the sense that whatever you did in the past is forgiven. And it actually feels like it's happening, because when I did it, it was just like someone had put his hand inside and taken everything out.'

After a time, Omar began to look for a wife. Arranged marriages are commonplace for Muslims, and so he told some friends of his desire to marry; and it so happened that a friend had another friend who had a relation in India who wanted a husband. Omar was shown a photograph of her. Before going to bed, he prayed a special prayer which translates something like this: 'If this thing is good for me, let it happen, and if it isn't, please keep it away from me.'

In time Omar's wife-to-be obtained a visa and came to England. He met her one Friday, and they exchanged greetings, although she spoke no English. Two days later they were married.

Omar's respect and love for, and pride in his wife and small daughter are very evident. When she arrived in this strange land to marry a strange man who spoke a strange language, he tried to ease the transition for her by learning as much as he could of her language, and equipping the kitchen with all the foods and cooking utensils with which she would have been familiar.

Her English is excellent now. I've only met her once because, as in many orthodox Muslim families, she stays at home most of the time. She doesn't like going out very much. She covers herself from head to foot in the traditional way. Omar explained that this is because 'the devil is in men, making them lustful'. So out of mutual respect, the women protect the men by keeping themselves separate from them, and covering their bodies.

To begin with, they lived, as Omar had done for nine years, on the Wirral. Then the landlord announced that they were 'unsuitable for the area'. It seemed sensible to move to the Granby area of Toxteth. After all, that was where all the Halal meat shops were, and the international grocery stores, and a Mosque.

I spent a morning in his shop recently. We had plenty of time to talk; business, as I said, is slow. He greeted his customers as old friends – and in a variety of languages, from Chinese and Arabic to Somali and Urdu. He has a smattering of several languages; enough for customer and shopkeeper to pass the time of day and do business. When he ran out of change, he said, 'Never mind – pay me tomorrow or when you're passing.'

We talked about the Muslim community. Many Muslims are not particularly strict. Some of Thomas' and Alexis' Muslim schoolfriends are not withdrawn from the Christian assemblies and occasional church services.

But many are as strict as they can be in their religious practices, which affect every aspect of life, from business and insurance to personal hygiene. Many local Muslims were born in Somalia and the Yemen. They came when the shipping trade was thriving.

There are two local Imams, and a strong, supportive community. Those who attend the Mosque tithe their wages and the money is used to benefit needy members of their community. Family ties are strong. The elderly are held in high esteem.

Many children attend Muslim school to learn the basics of the faith. There is an aggrieved sense of injustice that whereas Jews, Catholics and Anglicans have special schools, Muslims are not allowed to set up schools for the general education of their children. Muslim school is an after-school, strictly religious activity.

An elderly, bent, black-robed and veiled woman enters the shop, and tests the chillies between thumb and finger. She asks about some lamb, and the conversation continues, half in English and half in Arabic. She doesn't seem happy about the vegetables. Perhaps she remembers the days when she would have haggled over the prices. Omar is unhurried and courteous, and the old woman makes her purchases. I ask the price of the pistachio nuts. Omar grimaces. 'Don't ask!' he says. So I eye them wistfully and put away my purse.

We talk about the changes in Granby Street. Since the recent troubles, business has halved. Many shops have closed down. When I moved here in 1974, there was a small Tesco supermarket, there were clothes shops and butchers and bakers and fish shops, greengrocers, the Polish delicatessen, a dairy, cafés, take-aways, second-hand furniture shops, hardware stores . . .

Now there are a couple of Halal butchers, a few international grocery stores and a greengrocer, two or three newsagents and general stores, and, of course, a couple of betting shops and off-licences. Probably the most used shops which will be the last to go are the Post Office, the chemist, the barber's and the chandler's. In 1981, the wholesale confectionery store was burnt out. (We didn't forget that in a hurry, because an overpowering smell of burnt sugar hung in the air for weeks.) It's reopened as a sparsely stocked, but very friendly supermarket. I wonder how long it will be before it too follows the trend of so many Liverpool stores, and goes bankrupt.

An Egyptian customer has been propping up the counter for an hour or so. He's lived here for a few decades now. I ask him, and Omar, what they think the future is for Granby. They don't hesitate. There's no hope for Granby Street now. From a commercial point of view at least, it's dying.

We've had lots of recent cosmetic changes. New shop fronts and interiors, steel shutters, road resurfacing and newly laid pavements; and here and there, the ubiquitous cure-all tree-planting.

However, when there is heavy or persistent rainfall, gutters and drains overflow, and the pavements and roads become lakes and rivers. The zebra crossings on the nearby dual-carriageway, which we cross in order to go to school or to the shops or to church, disappear under several inches of water. I catch myself wondering how long such conditions would be tolerated in areas where people have money, and influence in high places. We have no option but to tolerate them, year in, year out.

A year or so ago, Granby shopkeepers began to meet together in order to give each other support, and to pool ideas. Some had had several burglaries; some had been subjected to various forms of intimidation. Some had been threatened with violence if they didn't keep their mouths shut about criminal activities they had unwillingly witnessed.

They drew up a list of changes that they would like to see implemented. Some delivery firms refuse to come into Granby Street, fearing that their loads will be lightened when their backs are turned. Of course, that's often precisely what does happen, if only by a loaf or a lemonade bottle or two, but occasionally in a rather more wholesale manner. It was recommended that the bollards at the dual-carriageway end of the street be removed, thus creating easier access. Nothing got changed. Disillusioned, the shopkeepers again resigned themselves to further losses in takings, little apparent hope of business picking up, and even less chance of starting afresh in a different area. Omar told me of a shop in the same block as his, with a large renovated flat above it. It was to be auctioned, with a reserve price of three thousand pounds.

I wondered what Omar could tell me about the protection rackets that I'd heard of, and how they affected shopkeepers. He said he knew nothing at all, and was sure that it was just part and parcel of the bad name that the Granby area of Toxteth has been given (not entirely without reason).

I had little evidence to support what I had heard. It may

well be just another of the rumours that are spread, dragging an already fallen community deeper into the dirt. There's no doubt that the media, in all their forms, find Toxteth, and especially Granby, a lucrative source of news.

We've got used to television crews, photographers and journalists. We don't give them a very warm welcome. It's all too easy to walk into a district, pick on the most eccentric in appearance, or the most garrulous onlookers, and hang an article or a programme around a few questionable gems gleaned from the local self-appointed philosophers. Of the various programmes I've seen or heard relating to Toxteth, all have had elements of truth, but certainly not the whole truth, and so the picture is inevitably distorted.

That was why we turned away the BBC television documentary crew who wanted to film a women's meeting a couple of years ago. There had been 'trouble in Granby', and a sizeable number of local mothers had gathered spontaneously, motivated largely by fear and anger, and had marched down to the local police station to express their grievances, and their fears for their children.

Subsequent meetings were held, and a handful of women volunteered to express our concerns to a police committee, thus opening up what was (perhaps inevitably) a short-lived dialogue.

The BBC's representative was very persuasive. She assured us that it would be a sympathetic report. The documentary, when it was televised, was to be entitled 'Voices from the Ghetto'. Well, we didn't want our voices recorded. The message from the representative was that it would be in our interests to let the BBC film us – it would give a better balance to the programme. (I rather fancy that they jeopardised any chance of our believing them when they gave the programme that particular title. Call a place a ghetto, and it's very hard to try to persuade outsiders that it isn't. The name sticks like super-glue. It rubs salt into a wound.)

Meanwhile, we remained sceptical of the favour that the BBC were, apparently, bestowing on us. It wasn't a favour that we had looked for, or needed. We were uncertain enough about our own understanding of our objectives, and we didn't want to work them out in front of a camera; only to have them reinterpreted by TV editors, and further dissected (or worse, ignored) by millions of viewers.

In 1981, there were scores of journalists and film crews in the area. Stephen was waylaid one afternoon by a French TV crew. Shortly afterwards, a friend's father, who lives in Paris, phoned his daughter to tell her that he'd just seen Stephen on his television, answering questions about the Toxteth riots. Our one claim to international fame!

If I possibly can, I ask journalists why they are here, and who they represent. (Other residents don't bother to ask. They simply remove the camera from the photographer's shoulder, and walk off with it.) I was particularly concerned the day a television crew were filming our children as they left school. It was an invasion of our privacy against which we were powerless to make effective protest.

So it wasn't surprising when the young woman who came into Omar's shop, just when I'd asked him about policing in the area, turned to me and abruptly demanded to know if I was one of the Dutch journalists who had, apparently, been around asking questions the previous weekend. Once I'd established my less exotic identity, she relaxed, and we thought we recognised each other after all, and, at Omar's suggestion, she told me of a distressing encounter she had had with local police.

A year or so ago, Elaine had gone out into the street to investigate what appeared to be a fight involving two women, telling her eight year old son to stay inside. Police arrived on the scene, and Elaine went to meet a man friend who was coming to her home for a meal. As they returned, they passed the scene of the fight and the two policemen.

At this point in the narrative, Elaine looked embarrassed. 'Do you mind if I swear?' she asked me. I told her that I didn't. She continued, 'The police said to me, "F - ing get home, you bitch." ' (I've heard similar things myself. It's sadly not at all exaggerated. In fact, it's often racist too.)

Things got a little confused at this point, at least in my understanding of events. But Elaine appears to have been hit in the face by one of the policemen, and heard her son repeatedly screaming, 'Don't hit my mum, don't hit my mum.' She was arrested, and charged with being drunk and disorderly, a charge that she denied.

Subsequently she was released, and appeared in court a month or two later. Several charges were levelled against her, the most serious of which was that she had been assaulting one of the policemen, beating him about the head.

The judge looked at the slight figure before him. 'Stand up,' he said to Elaine. He turned to the policeman. 'Are you sure that this is the defendant?' he asked him. He was sure. The judge addressed Elaine. 'How tall are you?' 'Five feet two,' she replied. The judge found it impossible to believe that Elaine had 'jumped up in the air and beaten this policeman', a burly six-footer. The case was dismissed.

'And from that day to this,' added Elaine, 'the same police walk along here, and they always look at me, and say, "Bitch".' As a child, she had liked and respected the police.

Omar chipped in. 'After the 1985 "riots", the police admitted they'd done wrong. They were swearing at people, "You black bastards, come on, we want a fight." They just beat everybody. Even if a man was standing in a doorway just watching, they pushed him on the floor.' You see a lot through a shop window.

He told us of the occasion on which a police superintendent had mistaken him for a plain-clothes policeman. He assured the superintendent that he wasn't, and they fell to discussing the problems of policing Toxteth, and Granby particularly. The superintendent told Omar that he wouldn't allow some of the men in his charge on to these streets, 'because they are so racist. And we can't do a thing about it. They just go out to harass people, and we know they do it, but we can't stop it.'

I don't need to tell you that this is by no means universally typical in the police force. Until I came to Toxteth, I had only had pleasant encounters with policemen and women. Personally speaking, that remains my experience, although some have asked me on different occasions, 'Why does a "nice girl" like you live in a place like this?'

Stephen had the singularly unpleasant experience of finding himself up against a riot shield not so long ago. There was a house raid in the next street, and he wanted to join Christian friends in a nearby house to pray for the situation. His way was barred by a policeman in full riot gear, plus all the weight of the authority which he represented. It gave Stephen an unexpected appreciation of the anger and sense of outrage which rioters experience – or which may incite people to riot.

Nevertheless, as a house-to-house survey in the Granby area showed, the majority of people here are fully in favour of policing. The one complaint – echoed again and again – was that people felt that the policing was too heavy-handed and aggressive. The police, understandably, defend their high-profile presence under most circumstances. They have had experiences of answering an emergency call to a shop or a house, only to be beaten up on arriving there. Brutal attacks have been made on them in broad daylight. The hatred many people feel for them is undisguised.

We've reached an unhappy stalemate. Many people accuse the community policemen and women, now back on the beat, of doing absolutely nothing. But if they do act, they are no longer trusted. Time and again, people complain that they had to wait for an hour or more for an answer to an emergency 999 call.

The police, for their part, hate having to come on duty here. Many people have told me that it's not local people who are troublemakers, but criminals and hooligans and (especially) joy-riding car thieves, who come into Granby from right outside Toxteth, believing that it is a 'no-go' area, and therefore a safe refuge. So we have more than our share of crime, and all that goes with it. Whether Granby is a 'no-go' area or not is a moot point. In theory it isn't, but in practice it often appears to be.

Like the rest of us, the police are fallible, fallen human beings. Most of us could recount stories of police helpfulness and kindness; some of true heroism and valour. I teach my sons that they should look on the police as their protectors, and that they are to be respected. I hope that they won't have to revise their opinions later.

It may sound as if I have deliberately dwelt on unpleasant accounts of police activity; but it has been my experience over the years that many people I've recounted similar incidents to refuse to believe that the police could be involved in racial abuse or bullying or deception. I could tell you many more stories similar to Elaine's. Two or three local Christians (sometimes identifiable by the clerical collars they were wearing at the time), have been roughly treated by police because they were talking to local black youths, or black community elders.

Yet many of these incidents are not officially reported. For a variety of reasons (not altogether clear to me, but obviously very real to those involved), many people – especially blacks – are afraid to sign their names at the bottom of the complaints form, thus invalidating their statements.

A massive breakdown in our relationship with the police has occurred – one which demands radical treatment. Like Elaine, most local young adults liked and respected the police when they were children. The breakdown is a recent phenomenon, it would seem. There is mistrust on many sides, and more significantly, perhaps, there is a growing decline in respect for authority, particularly when it is associated with the Establishment. And the police epitomise that kind of authority. They are going to have to earn all over again the respect that they once took for granted, as are many others who have taken their authority for granted.

Yet again, another pile of questions and problems, and no corresponding pile of answers and solutions. Back in Omar's shop, none of us needs reminding that, even if we phrase it differently, we are all weak and sinful by nature. But we don't all see eye-to-eye on the remedy.

7

Voices

One step towards a remedy, suggested from various quarters, is that opportunity should be given to enable people in inner-cities to voice their experiences of life and its living. Acting on ideas put forward in the Archbishop of Canterbury's *Faith in the City* report, churches in Toxteth and Aigburth were issued with leaflets and some very basic questions relating to housing, health, work, money, schools and worship. People were encouraged to fill them in, anonymously if they wished. There were two further sections to write on, under the headings: 'My biggest hopes and wishes', and 'My biggest worries and fears for the future'.

Following the exercise, there was a discussion on the findings. Some while later there was a further meeting. It was this one that I attended, because it was in a local church hall.

I jokingly remarked beforehand that I guessed that it would be a very middle-class gathering, with lots of people with a professional interest in Toxteth, but who lived elsewhere; and no local residents. To my intense dismay, I was practically right on target. I almost turned round and went back home, but overcame my prejudice and stayed.

To be fair, one or two local people did eventually come, and there was at least one of the 'professionals' who lived, as well as worked, in Granby. And the rest were sincerely concerned with the problems facing inner-city dwellers. But I came away feeling that, had we stayed all night, we wouldn't have been much nearer to effecting any grass-roots changes. This kind of talk is cheap. It's action that costs.

Again the idea was put forward: give people a voice; get

them to come together like this, and talk. Or go into the pubs and clubs and get them to talk.

But, even assuming that the general principle has some merit, it just isn't as easy as that. The mothers' meetings I mentioned in the last chapter effectively demonstrate this. We had an initial common cause: fear for the safety, short- and long-term, of our children. The first problem was to get people to talk at all (after the immediate drama of the first spontaneous gathering had passed).

There were a few natural spokespeople and leaders, but no one else was inclined to speak publicly – they would to their friends, but not in a large meeting. There wasn't much structure to the meetings, although a chairperson was usually elected.

So to begin with the natural talkers dominated, and after one or two meetings others who held differing opinions did one of two things: dared to open their mouths to disagree, or stopped coming.

Now a further problem developed; those with the strongest views, often those whose surfacing anger and frustration made them articulate, had begun to mould the direction of the meetings, so a rather militant atmosphere developed. And the more reserved women stopped coming, feeling out of their depth, unable to understand or identify with some of the views that had been expressed, and finding the atmosphere rather too aggressive and threatening. After a few meetings, the whole thing simply atrophied.

'Getting people to talk' certainly isn't a panacea for social discontent, although it has its value. Give someone a voice, and, once they've found how to use it, they have an astonishing amount to say – on just about everything.

Our meetings were about children and about policing. But every imaginable topic and grievance was aired. Once the flood-gate was opened, everything poured out.

Discussion groups, as most people elsewhere understand

them, are rather cerebral affairs. Logic and reason are essential ingredients, or, at least, we can certainly appeal to them. But the people who are being encouraged to 'talk' in inner cities, for example, live in a far less cerebral and forward thinking way than the professionals who encourage the discussion. Life here is altogether more governed by emotion, and the immediacy of a need or the primary response to a situation may be the motivating factor for taking action, rather than a more considered and reasoned response.

Thus, passion is unleashed in discussions, and people become excitable and emotional, and misunderstandings easily arise. Opening up like this tends to make people at once vulnerable and impassioned, and if someone expresses a contrary or alternative point of view, it's all too easy to feel hurt, threatened or rejected. This again often leads to a defensive, angry reaction. Many people don't have the vocabulary which they need to express all they're feeling (which is why expletives are often necessary as release valves); so they may appear to ramble, or repeat themselves, or perhaps misuse words, thus confusing issues (and probably themselves).

Bringing our fears and hopes, our anger and ambitions, our problems and dreams into the open, can be a good and creative experience, especially when they're tossed around and explored and developed within a group where there is mutual trust and respect. But we need to be wary of advocating discussion groups or 'talk-ins' as a way of problem solving. It may be that they become the vehicle for unleashing lots of fear, anger, frustration, resentment, disillusionment . . . which simply hangs heavily over the group, sometimes transferring to others, and in fact not being dealt with at all.

It's as if a surgeon opens someone up, exposes the diseased organs, and then walks away. Or tells the patient to complete the job herself. What is needed instead is an opportunity to give, and to receive, forgiveness, healing and love.

The New Testament writer James wrote, 'Everyone should be quick to listen, slow to speak and slow to become angry, for man's anger does not bring about the righteous life God desires' (James 1.19–20). We need to consider carefully our motives for, and the consequences of, 'giving people a voice'. But that is not an excuse for not working towards that end.

It's been an education for me, listening to the voices of people who've been brought up around Granby. Hannah and Ron, for example, opened my eyes to things I've never experienced, and wouldn't be able to write about with any authority. I almost wished it was a public setting when Ron and I talked – or rather, Ron talked and I listened – because the power of his words affected me deeply.

Both black, they were born and raised around Granby. Hannah's grandparents came over from Sierra Leone. She has two daughters who are at school with Thomas and Alexis. She's separated from their father, although the girls stay with him from time to time.

I met Hannah at a typing class, and then wondered how I'd managed not to meet her earlier; she's never on her own, and seems to know everyone, and is altogether a delightful person.

Ron is in his early thirties. Among other things, he opened my eyes to the conflicting pressures and choices facing a black Christian from Toxteth. He enabled me to appreciate, in a small measure, the Church's inability, in his experience, to give him wise and discerning advice which would help him to come to terms with, and resolve, those dilemmas.

His father came from Jamaica with recruitments for the RAF. His mother is Scottish, and has three sons from a previous marriage. So Ron has three half-brothers and four sisters.

Both he and Hannah went to local schools. Ron feels he

was an under-achiever, because of home pressures; his parents were constantly fighting and so they separated, and he would live first with one, and then with the other, and found it all very stressful. Finally they divorced and he lived, reluctantly, with his mother. He was taken out of the home for a while because of hassles between his mother and her boyfriends.

Hannah also remembers feeling confused about her identity at school. One teacher told her, 'You've got a chip on your shoulder, because you don't know if you're black or white.' Years later, while visiting friends in London, she heard herself described as a 'red-skin'. Although it may be considered a compliment, and a sign of beauty, Hannah interpreted it to mean that, because you're neither fully black nor white, 'you're not full pedigree, you're just a mongrel'.

Ironically, although both Hannah's parents were fully black, she has the lighter colouring of someone of mixed race, which has caused confusion at times. She would love one day to go to Africa. 'I've always wanted to go; there was a sort of pull.' That yearning to go, she explained, was independent of any experience of racism.

Her parents are content to stay in Britain. They don't talk of issues concerning racism. Ron also found this in his father, 'He was more English than an Englishman. It's us second- and third-generation blacks who have the attitude that, whereas our parents and grandparents were passive in their attitude towards racism, we are active.' He added that he felt for himself it should be 'all the more so, as a Christian, without getting out of order'.

How much, I wondered, did issues concerning race affect him? 'If the tables were turned and the white community were in the minority,' Ron thought, 'they'd be surprised at how much they think about it – racism, colour – themselves.' He added that he couldn't say how much he consciously thought about it all, but that it was probably a lot more than he'd assumed, and that we'd all probably be surprised if we were able to document it.

He recalled one of the first times he became aware of colour. He was about six at the time, and a programme of pop music came on the television. 'I remember running in and saying, "Oh, I hope there's a black group on." Now this is TV almost twenty-four years ago, hardened BBC, stiff-upper-lip, and they had the occasional black face flashed on, but I was inherently aware of it even then, though I wasn't able to articulate what I was missing.' And he would experience a sense of joyful identification when, as on this occasion, a black group was shown.

'Racism', thought Hannah, 'happens where people are ignorant.' She told me about a nursery school she had worked in as an assistant in Scotland ('Scottie') Road, one of Liverpool's most famous – or infamous – districts. Like the majority of Liverpool, much of Toxteth included, it is an almost exclusively white area.

All the people at Hannah's school were white, except two: Hannah herself ('I was the only black person that had ever worked there') and one little Arab girl, 'And she stood out, and everyone would say, "Ahhh, look at her," like she was something different.'

And the myths which perpetuate racism and other prejudice continue to flourish. 'If anything came on the radio about Granby Street,' Hannah remembered, 'they'd be like that: "Oooh, I believe there were riots, and everyone had guns!" They don't understand, and it's probably the same as goes on in Scottie Road.' She considered a little, and added, 'Maybe they think black people are animals, crowds of them everywhere.'

She spoke without bitterness, but rather as if she were trying to put herself into their shoes, to see what it looked like from their point of view. One day, she brought a friend from work home with her, and they walked down Granby Street.

Hannah grinned as she described her friend's amazement at seeing so many black people. Back at work, she told her workmates, 'I've just walked down Granby Street.' 'And,' said Hannah, 'the people in work said, "Why? Why did you go down there? You could have been killed! You're stupid going down there." ' As it happens, Hannah's friend now spends almost as much time in Granby as she does in Scottie Road.

In rather more sophisticated ways, many have had similar reactions to my living here. Some balk at the dereliction, others seem angered at what they consider to be the indolence of those who hang around on the streets, others are scared by rumours (not unfounded, but not understood) of violence. More striking, perhaps, is not so much their lack of comprehension – that is understandable – as their lack of compassion. It's so easy to sit in judgement and to pronounce solutions to problems at a distance.

For now, Hannah is happy enough for her children to be living in Granby, although she doesn't let them play out, for, as she says, 'I probably wouldn't let them play out anywhere else – there's a lot of nasty things going on in the world.' Looking to the future, though, she hopes that they will leave Liverpool. 'There's nothing for them, only YTS schemes and things like that, and can you imagine what it's going to be like in another ten years?'

In Ron and Hannah and many others, there's a sense of deep loyalty to Granby. Toxteth as a whole is probably like many other inner cities, sharing similar problems. But Granby is different, Granby is isolated in the middle. It's where young black people in particular feel at home; for some, the only place they feel comfortable in. Those without jobs will come into the area, if they live outside it, just to spend the day in a congenial atmosphere.

Nevertheless, it's an oppressive atmosphere too, and there is what I can best describe as an aura of anger and hurt and despair that I haven't felt anywhere else. I become conscious of it when I'm out of the place, and it's like a weight lifted from my back.

Ron and Hannah have both experienced life outside Toxteth, Ron for long periods of time. When, or if, the time does come for Hannah's daughters to leave, she will be in a position to give them encouragement and advice. For most, though, it's the impossible dream. For where can you go without money, or qualifications, or self-confidence? If Granby – an area that takes up a very little space on a map of the city – is the only place where you can find your identity, it's easy to see how the atmosphere can become oppressive, and tension can mount, and troubles break out. If Granby becomes the ghetto that many consider it to be already, it will be in part due to the animosity of much of the rest of Toxteth, let alone the rest of the city, which shuns and disowns it.

Ron was accused more than once by fellow Christians of having a 'ghetto mentality'. 'Get out of it,' they would say. 'And if I get out of it,' he asked, 'what do I become?' He described the time he'd gone back from church one evening and wept. 'I was really crying to the Lord, really knotted up inside, and saying how I *refuse* to become a white man just to go on with God. I told him I wasn't prepared to prostitute my being for other people's opinions.' Such opinions, he declared, had no intrinsic worth or value, and were not founded on anything he would enter into.

What was it his Christian friends were asking him to do, and why? It seemed ultimately that they were asking him to cut away his roots, in order to become more like themselves. Why, thought Ron, should his memories of living in what they called the ghetto be of less value than theirs? Because it was tough, did it invalidate it all? On the contrary, his struggles gave him strength and insights into hardship that his middle-class fellow churchgoers knew little about.

'They're saying, turn from the "ghetto" to – what? To

suburbia?' The result would be his adoption of middle-class values and attitudes which, he was sure of, 'have nothing whatsoever to do with Christianity'.

Alongside the 'ghetto mentality' label is the tired old 'chip on the shoulder'. I sat in a seminar recently, where the issues of Christian attitudes towards racism were being tossed around. My heart sank as a bright, intelligent young white man threw out the question, 'Don't you think that they [black people] have a chip on their shoulder?'

Ron described how he had run a barber's shop in Bradford for a few years, and had gone to a Restoration church there. The few other black Christians in the congregation all had as much internal turmoil as he did, he said. But his was 'a bit more volatile' than theirs. So he was told that he had a chip on his shoulder.

That, as far as Ron is concerned, is 'the biggest cop-out'. He has thought deeply about it, and concluded that 'the majority of people who tell you that are those most inadequate at coping with what you're saying.' Why? 'Because it relieves them of any responsibility to consider that possibly they *may* be wrong, that there *may* be a bigger issue here.'

Circumstances have forced Ron to live away from Toxteth at the moment. Articulate and resourceful, he's never at a loose end. But there's a restless energy, a touch of the crusader about him as he searches for the way to express his God-given identity.

He became a Christian at the age of twenty while serving a three-year prison sentence for robbery. He found himself one week in solitary confinement. During that time he had nothing else to do but sit, think and read. He read the Bible and some religious books he was allowed to take with him which had been given to him by Christian acquaintances. He read *The Cross and the Switchblade*. And thus began what he describes as his 'tempestuous love affair with Jesus'.

Not an 'average churchgoer', he knew nothing of doctrine,

or the history of Christianity. He learnt alone, reading the Bible and literature given him by a nun who worked in the prison. There were infrequent visits from the chaplain, distant because of the sheer pressure of numbers.

Although he missed out on teaching and fellowship, he saw the benefit of 'not being interfered with; you're not tainted with so much that's around in Christianity that's got nothing to do with Christianity'.

When he finished his prison sentence, he joined a succession of different churches outside Toxteth. That isn't as odd as it may appear. There isn't a local church with a strong black presence, although most (not all) local congregations have a few black members. However, most of them are culturally very different from Ron, and often much older, with different values and traditions and outlooks.

He feels at home where there is a charismatic orientation, and where the worship and structure are informal. Excepting one local, long-established house church (which has its own distinct style and mode of worship, and where one quickly becomes aware of what is and is not 'acceptable' behaviour), there isn't a local church where Ron would naturally feel at home.

And soon he faced another pressure from the churches he attended: to get out of Toxteth. The reason that he was given was that God wanted to 'prosper' him. That's fine, he thought, but I don't see why God can't prosper me in Toxteth.

No one would give him an intelligent reason for moving out. He found that the Christians he knew were insular, tending to mix mainly with other Christians. He knew people from all kinds of backgrounds, yet he felt he was being pressured to become part of 'this little cocoon', which didn't give him any real social or intellectual satisfaction.

And there was prejudice. There had been much talk in one church about the community of God's people, and of love and unity. One day, while out jogging, Ron cut his foot badly on a broken bottle, and had to stay at home in his bed-sitter in Toxteth for over three weeks while it healed. He got word to members of his church, which he attended regularly – 'I was a *tithing* church member.' During that time, not one of them came to visit him.

It was his old friends – the same ones, he said, whom his church friends 'looked down their noses at' – who came to visit him. He had one friend who had burgled him eighteen months earlier, who came and brought food and cooked it for Ron. Others came too, willing to shop and cook and clean. 'These,' he told me, 'are the same people out burgling houses; they're the same people I used to go doing armed robberies and muggings with.' I can't help recalling the parable of the Good Samaritan.

The prejudice had a racist face too. A black elder of a church confided in him how the parents of a young woman in his congregation, all of whom were charismatic Christians, had told her never to date, or bring home, a coloured man. Ron asked the elder how it made him feel, and he described how difficult he finds it each week when these people come to church with their daughter, and shake his hand, 'and everything's rosy and good'.

Ron himself tries to be as civil to those and other white Christians he knows to have racist attitudes (like the young man who, in a tense moment during a card game, called him a 'black idiot'), but the strain is great. He pictured a typical after-church conversation: ' "How are you doing?" "Great, everything's fine!" "Praise the Lord!" I *can't* go through with that – you're insulting me – forget about everything else, morals, God, Jesus, it's an insult. And I'm expected to continue the façade.'

He told me how he had tried standing on principle over issues that were important to him, and how it had cost him dearly. Both of us wondered how Christians had failed in the past, and were still failing, to relate to one another, especially when colour or culture differ.

At the simplest level, Ron told me it's just a matter of people being alongside people. How do you talk to anyone? But, he continued, it's not coming through. 'Christians produce offspring of their own kind. They are not around the areas where they can touch the likes of people like me.'

Remember, Ron found his faith inside the four walls of a prison cell, not in the heart of Toxteth. He's learnt to cope with the occasionally excruciating insensitivity of his fellow Christians because he loves, and is loved by, the same God whom they love.

At the moment, he's not sure which church to attend. He felt increasingly stifled by the suburban churches where there seemed to be fewer and fewer points of contact, and more and more pressure for him to become 'one of them'. He longs to move back into Toxteth, into Granby; but it's tough for an ex-con who wants no dealings with the sort of activities most of his friends are mixed up in. Yet he still feels closer to them than to any of his Christian sisters and brothers.

The evening he came to see me, he had first sat a while in his car, watching the drug pushers on Granby Street. It's to Granby that people from all over Merseyside come for marijuana. It saddened Ron to see how much energy these young men were putting into their business; creative, imaginative energy being used for a dead-end purpose. The police turn a blind eye to this drug dealing. Whether they gain the respect of the local community for doing so, I don't know. Too many incidents keep the fires of mistrust burning.

One day, I was talking to some friends about the police's perception of me as a well-spoken white woman, and how I never experience harassment from them, nor expect to, and how it was therefore hard for me to fully appreciate the experience of someone like Elaine, whom I'd met in Omar's store.

'I had a bad experience,' said Hannah suddenly. A few mornings later, she called round to tell me about it. Although normally very extrovert, she felt shy and unsure about talking about it. But she knew that I was writing about life in Toxteth, and she wanted other people to hear what had happened to her.

So, lighting the first of many cigarettes – she was visibly nervous – she had told me of the time her cousin John had come to stay with her.

John had, at seventeen, had a few brushes with the law. His step-brothers were known troublemakers, and he got tarred with the same brush. One day he was picked up by the police and accused of threatening a woman with a knife, and of stealing her money. He denied the charges, having been, he insisted, in another town at the apparent time of the attack.

He was given bail, and, with the permission of his solicitor, moved in with Hannah in order to be nearer to his mother, who was unwell.

One evening he, Hannah and the girls were decorating the living room, when they became aware of police activity over the back wall. 'Look,' they said, 'there's police hiding in that empty house.'

Shortly afterwards they went to bed, and were woken the next morning at seven o'clock by loud banging on the door. Hannah looked out of her window, and saw that her flat was surrounded by police and police dogs. They had (for what reason, she didn't know) waited all night to raid *her* home.

They waved a warrant at her, but she couldn't see the names on it. They had come, they said, for John. In order to find him, they 'turned the cupboards out, they turned the drawers out, they turned just everything out – knives, forks, dishes . . . ' And then they arrested both John and Hannah.

They took her daughters too. 'They got them out of bed. They began screaming. The coppers weren't nice to them – I

68

think that's what annoyed me most. They wouldn't let them get dressed. They walked through the streets with their nighties on.'

The memory seemed to distress her, and she suddenly felt cold. I made more coffee, and she continued the story.

The rest of the day had been taken up with several periods of questioning. She and the girls were put in a room with benches round the wall, but no toilet. Later in the morning, a friend was contacted to come and collect the girls. She didn't know what had happened to John, and the police asked no questions relating to him or his alleged crime.

She was asked several questions about various residents of Granby, though. And at six in the evening she was, without explanation, put in a police van and driven several times up and down Granby Street. Finally she was taken back to the station and her cell, where she remained overnight.

'I couldn't even go to the toilet, because there was dirt all up the walls.' She hadn't been since she got up that morning. 'They gave me a brawn sandwich, and a jam buttie, which I couldn't eat. I just wanted to go to the toilet.'

As far as I can see, there were no grounds for the charges brought against John and Hannah. Hannah was charged with receiving stolen goods, in the shape of a colour television. She has a black-and-white television, and knew nothing of any colour ones, stolen or otherwise. She was bewildered by the whole experience. Later, the charges were dropped.

The woman who had accused John of attacking her moved down to London, and the policemen who had arrested John after that attack were moved to London too. None of them turned up in court, and it left Hannah with a lot of questions, such as, 'If John *had* been threatening the woman, why should she go off like that? And why were the police moved? The Crown Court said even *they* couldn't get hold of them.'

The case was thrown out of court. There was no compensation. Had I endured an experience like that, I'm certain that I wouldn't have been the only one asking questions. Not so for Hannah and John. And most of their questions still remain unanswered.

Hannah's attitude is to try and shrug it all off. Just one or two comments which she let slip made me appreciate that she hasn't much affection any more for the police, or much faith in the courts.

Her daughters are afraid of the police now. Walking back from posting a letter one day, they witnessed a car chase, and suddenly there were lots of policemen about the place. The girls began screaming, 'The baddies, the baddies, they're going to get us!' It was the police they were pointing at.

At school, they play alongside Thomas and Alexis, for all the world as carefree a bunch of children as you might find anywhere. In reality, those little girls have experienced something which will scar them permanently, and it will take a great deal of persuasion to convince them that the police are on their side.

Ron, too, knows what it means to be on the wrong side of the law. He's done time for something he deserved to be punished for. That's in the past.

Now, he's a law-abiding, respectable citizen. But he's still black. Recently, he was driving his car through a white, middle-class area of Liverpool, on his way to church. Two policemen stopped him. He knew why. It had happened before. Here he was, a young black man, driving a car outside the known black territory – chances were it was a stolen car.

'You're a bit far from Liverpool 8, aren't you?' they asked him. With a sigh of despair he dropped his arms, and prayed involuntarily, 'Oh, Father.'

'What did you say?' demanded the policemen. They ordered him out of his car, and promptly arrested him, charging him with assault. They called him a variety of names, including coon, wog, nigger.

His church supported him in court, and the charges were dropped. But the insult doesn't fall away so easily.

8

Square Pegs

When I began to write this book I discovered the inadequacies of longhand, chief of which are (in my case) illegibility and writer's cramp. We have a portable typewriter, so I decided to join a typing class at the Methodist Centre to speed things up.

As it happens my longhand is still faster than my typing, but I can manage to type without looking at the keyboard (even if what comes up on the paper is often complete nonsense). The great pleasure, however, has been getting to know Geraldine Poole, the typing teacher. I've probably progressed rather slowly because so much of our lesson time has been taken up in conversation. We discovered that we share similar feelings about Toxteth.

One day, Gerry was asked to speak at a Women's World Day of Prayer meeting. People were obviously moved by what she said. They were fellow citizens of Liverpool, yet unaware until then of how thousands were struggling to survive only a bus ride away. She began:

I have lived all my life on the edge of Liverpool 8, but it is only in the last six years, while working there, that I have come to realise what I call 'the silent suffering' which exists there.

The area has become a ghetto. It may surprise some, as it did me, to know that many black people are actually afraid to travel on buses to certain parts of the city – for they know that they would not be welcome. Now, my grandparents came to Liverpool from Ireland – that means that just two generations ago, my family were not here. Yet no one questions the fact that I am here.

I can move about the city freely, I can confidently apply for jobs, I know I am accepted. Some black families in Liverpool have been here since the turn of the century – yet they are *still* having to fight for equal status, for equal opportunities and acceptance.

Gerry teaches at three centres for further education, with predominantly black students. When she first began her work, she felt self-conscious of her whiteness, and tried to play it down. She felt conspicuous not only because of her colour, but because her husband had not known unemployment, and because her three children are all heading for university with all its opportunities.

Having painted a picture of her own background, which mirrored that of the majority of women listening to her talk, Gerry went on to tell them about one of her students, Cynthia. 'Cynthia, to me,' said Gerry, 'epitomises how it *is* possible, through human suffering, to see the greatness of God's love for us all.'

Cynthia is a white woman in her mid-thirties, married to a black man. Such a marriage can lead to ostracism from both white and black communities. She has a son who is in care, and a daughter who may die at any time because of a brain haemorrhage. As if that wasn't enough, her husband is a stroke victim, confined to a chair by the fire in the living room. Because there's no room for one (let alone two) beds downstairs, Cynthia also sleeps on a chair in the living room, just to keep him company.

Some while ago, a stolen car careered through her back fence, stopping just short of her back door. Now the back of her house is quite unprotected, and vulnerable to attack. Rats frequently invade her home, and it makes no difference how clean she keeps the place.

Gerry met Cynthia when she enrolled in one of her typing classes, and that's where I met her some time later. Gerry recognised potential in her, and encouraged her to enrol for a full-time general education course.

'If you were to meet Cynthia,' said Gerry, 'you would be impressed by a quietly spoken, gentle, caring woman. She never raises her voice or loses her temper.' Gerry added that she felt that she had learnt more from Cynthia than from many of her own teachers.

Cynthia is small and slight, almost frail; she looks as if she hasn't enough time to take care of herself properly. But that was the only clue to her story. Had I not heard Gerry give her talk, I wouldn't have known of the grimness of Cynthia's circumstances.

Gerry estimates that at least half of her time is taken up with trying to convince people that they *can* achieve educationally. 'Many', she explained, 'have gone through an education system which expected little from them, and so they expected little from themselves.'

The course that Cynthia enrolled for has just been cut from a year to eighteen weeks. So now, said Gerry, in eighteen short weeks, 'we have to try and lift our students from an attitude of hopelessness to one of optimism and hope'.

Cynthia has impressed me with her ambition to be a teacher. My heart sinks at the thought of what she would have to go through to realise her goal; GCEs, interviews, entry into the academic world of a teacher training college. Frankly, as things stand, she would be a square peg in a round hole. But that will be education's greater loss. What a richness of life experience Cynthia has to offer – what enthusiasm, what lessons in perseverance, in overcoming. Should she choose to carry on to that end, then just so long as there are teachers like Gerry around to help her, she may make it.

The school system didn't work for Cynthia. Needless to say, there are plenty like her. Just so long as funding is available, Gerry and her colleagues will find plenty of work to do.

One of the benefits of the Women's Movement has been to awaken women, especially working-class women, to see that they must have more to offer and more to receive than the traditional domestic roles that many drift into. So, rather than sit around in boredom, often alongside unwaged boyfriends or husbands, they enrol in local classes to pick up their education again.

It's usually a more stimulating education, relevant to their experience of life. It may be black studies, or politics, or developing writing skills. Some may study 'O' levels, such as maths or English. For some, it leads on to other opportunities, further education, even a course preparatory to university entrance. For others there may even be a chance of paid employment.

A chance to start again. It's very encouraging. But why didn't it happen first time around? Why did they fail in the usual education system; how did the system fail them? Is education in the inner city so different from education anywhere else?

Nowadays most small children make an enthusiastic start to school. In Toxteth, most children make an early start, too, from as young as two years old in playgroups, and most begin their full-time education at nursery school when they are three.

I realise how fortunate we have been in our children's pre-schooling when I hear of the lengthy waiting lists many children have to work their way through, and of various other restrictions which make entry into playgroups seem like entry into a secret society for which no one ever tells you the password.

Thomas and Alexis both attended the Methodist Centre playgroup, just around the corner. The emphasis, under the various leaders, was on educational play. Most children understood the play bit quickly enough. And the educational side developed too. 'If I bite John, he will scream because he doesn't like it. That is not, therefore, the way to get the toy I want from John. I don't like smacks.'

An informal atmosphere was cultivated at the playgroup. So parents felt free to drop off their children when it was convenient for them, and to collect them more or less in time for lunch. Activities were organised for the mothers too, ranging from keep-fit and swimming to typing classes and shopping trips.

Several of the parents who have made use of the playgroup over the years are over in the UK to study, and English isn't their first language. Generally, the father's English is better than the mother's, which is sometimes practically non-existent. The children overcome the language barrier quite quickly. After all, they're still developing their language skills, and soon pick up what they need to know to get by. Many homes are bilingual, and the children speak Scouse by day and, perhaps, Malay by night.

When they are three, most children move up to nursery school. Thomas and Alexis attended different ones. Their primary school doesn't have nursery facilities (though not for lack of effort on the part of the school governors in trying get the necessary space made available over the years).

Alexis attended the nursery department of the local Roman Catholic school. The priest and headmaster were quite happy that we weren't Catholics, and said that religious education didn't begin until the children started in the infant school. I remember walking through the park, with Alexis skipping and hopping along, singing and chanting to himself. All of a sudden he recited a word-perfect 'Hail Mary', and then launched into some nursery rhyme, almost in the same breath. (Our church is conservative Evangelical.)

I loved collecting him in the winter months. A delicious smell of hot buttered toast wafted out through the classroom door. A much cosier alternative to orange squash and biscuits, the usual mid-morning snack.

At this stage of education, things seem to be much alike everywhere else. Joyce Grenfell's monologues would be as enlightening about Toxteth nursery school life as they would about Surrey's nursery school activities. In fact, I'd recommend them before any other educational work to anyone wanting an accurate picture of pre-school education.

We were unusually spoilt for choice when it came to choosing a primary school. Apart from the local Catholic primary school, we could have found places in any one of five other schools within walking distance of our house. We chose the Church of England school affiliated to our sister church. It had a reputation for high standards of behaviour, which we were sure Thomas and Alexis could benefit from.

There's a friendly, family atmosphere in the infant department, and, by and large, the staff appear to be very committed to their work. Unlike me at that age, Thomas and Alexis enjoyed their first years at school.

Junior school, though, hasn't been a smooth ride for Thomas. Discipline seems harder to maintain. Children begin losing their natural openness with their teachers; they don't chat to them and confide in them so much, and they start to form their friendship groups and gangs. He has had an especially hard year, being in one of the hardest to discipline lower-junior classes that the staff can remember. The new teacher who took them for the first term found it too much, and handed in her resignation. A tough class in Toxteth is a tough class. Nevertheless, after that hiccup, and with a more experienced teacher in charge, things have taken a smoother course.

My overall impression (I can't give a professional assessment) of teachers in Toxteth primary schools is that they are, by and large, exceptionally dedicated and caring. That isn't to say that they are always the most skilled teachers, and some teaching methods appear outdated or inappropriate. Yet it's clear that many teachers love

(I choose the word 'love' deliberately) their pupils.

Where links have been forged between staff, parents and community, there is an exceptionally strong educational unit. You have to give a lot of yourself in an inner-city school; if you are prepared to do that, there are plenty of rewards. At least, that's the message I receive from local teachers.

Sometimes the pressure is too much. I was told of supply teachers sent into local primary schools who left after as short a period as a morning. A head teacher Stephen taught under some years ago suffered a nervous breakdown.

One teacher was at a meeting where a local community worker stood up and announced, 'The education standards and the teachers in the inner city are hopeless.' 'Excuse me,' said the teacher, 'but I teach just around the corner. Are you telling me that I'm a hopeless teacher?' He evaded the question. 'The middle-class schools, like X for example, have got all the best teachers,' was his reply. 'I taught at X, as a matter of fact, before I came to this school,' said the teacher. 'Are you telling me that I was a good teacher while I was at X, but have become a hopeless one since I moved here?' The community worker consulted his watch and announced that it was lunch-time.

The teacher in question finds Toxteth a much more challenging, and therefore stimulating, atmosphere to work in than her previous post. Certainly, with such an ethnic variety as we have in our particular neighbourhood, children grow up with a far richer infusion of colour and culture than there is in many British communities, which is a tremendous advantage. If they develop racist attitudes, ignorance is unlikely to be the excuse.

In Granby Street school, eighty-two per cent of the children are from ethnic minorities, representing about sixteeen different ethnic origins (including Liverpool-born blacks). In our boys' school, although there is a bigger percentage of white children, there are eighteen different ethnic backgrounds. The biggest ethnic groups in Granby Street school are Chinese, Liverpool-born blacks, and Somalis. There are Hindus, Muslims and Rastafarians; children of all religions and none. The attitude towards religion in the school was described to me by a worker in the Parent Centre as 'live and let live'.

Parent Centres have sprung up in several schools throughout the inner-city area. There are officially appointed workers who liaise with both the school and the community, but the Centres are designed so as to be more or less organised and run by the parents (and grandparents and other friends) who come along.

All sorts of classes and courses may be on offer, as interests or talents show themselves, ranging from sports and pottery to local history and calligraphy. In Granby Parent Centre, some of the fathers made toys for the toddlers' room. They saw similar ones advertised in an educational toys' catalogue, and proceeded to make them themselves at a fraction of the price.

So the loyalty to the school often evident among the staff spills over to the parents, and filters out to the community. One Centre has been used by an eighty year old grandmother (who attends a weekly bingo session there), and visited by the forty-eight hours old baby of one of the regular parents, who dropped into the Centre on her way home from hospital (having gone into labour in the Centre in the first place!).

Education, of course, covers so many areas not actually written into the curriculum. Happily, educational material is considerably more enlightened in its awareness of sexist and racial and class stereotyping than it was a decade or so ago.

Schools need increasingly to take on board the challenge of sexism. The imbalance of the overwhelming majority of primary (especially infant) school teachers being women seems hard to change. It is significant, however, that the majority of headteachers are men. In an area where up to fifty per cent of the pupils are from one-parent families, and that parent is invariably the mother, there is a need for men to figure positively in children's lives. When I left teacher training college in 1974, only two male students in the college were intending to look for posts in infant departments. The evidence since then doesn't suggest much change.

Gender stereotyping, of course, starts very early. Around here, baby girls are often over-dressed in acres of pink frills, and their slightly older sisters totter along in miniature versions of their mothers' fashions: mini-mini skirts, leather boots or fur coats (doubtless the only size fur coat that could be afforded). Eight or nine year olds wear lipstick and nail varnish, and talk about being 'in love' with male rock music idols and the stars of adult TV shows.

There's much to be concerned about in educational policies towards racism, too. The LEA has issued a code of practice to each teacher in the Authority, outlining ways of combating racist behaviour.

Some teachers told me that their policy is to ignore racist remarks made by the children to one another, rather than draw attention to them. But if no action is taken, then the result is reinforcement by silence. Children usually *do* know what it is they're saying, and silence may well be taken to signify approval. And any name-calling, be it 'wog' or 'paki' or 'fatty', needs to be effectively dealt with, not ignored.

It can be hard, veering to impossible, for schools to keep up with educational material. Resources in all schools are low, and getting lower. Yet books are especially important in areas like Toxteth, where very few families have well-stocked bookshelves, and not many make regular use of the library services.

Stephen discovered that inner-city infant and junior children's preference for reading schemes ran contrary to the experts' predictions. 'Instead of the specially written stories featuring run-down terraces and high-rise blocks, inhabited by "true-to-life" characters, the pupils would choose for themselves the old "Janet and John" series, and even the maligned Ladybird schemes.' The most popular reading scheme, he found, was Sheila McCullagh's 'Pirate' fantasies, which at the time seemed unique in acknowledging that young children already have a developed sense of humour.

In the curriculum generally, Stephen was frustrated by the lack of 'anything other than a deadly seriousness' in the teaching material which, after all, often bores the teacher, let alone his or her pupils.

He taught for some years in a purpose-built semi-open-plan primary school. It was a teacher's nightmare. All the classrooms were built to the minimum size specifications (to economise) and were simply too small. The walls, where they existed, were paper-thin, and contained some of the hardest to discipline pupils in the country. (This is the school that made national headlines a few years ago because of 'rioting'.) The staff had permanent headaches. The huge picture windows meant that the place became like a furnace during the summer. And they were as good as a cinema screen. Passing parents came up to bang on them to attract their offspring's attention, sometimes signing them to come over so that they could talk directly to them. Other children – the ones playing truant – came over to squash their faces against the glass, to the pupils' great amusement. And the packs of semi-wild alsatians bounded over and leapt up, barking joyously at potential playmates (or quarries).

And of course, an open-plan building, with its low, flat roofs, huge windows, and low-cost building materials, is much easier to break and enter than a fortified Victorian plant. Nevertheless, experience has taught Granby Street school (which is over a hundred years old) to place wire grilles over its windows. It's disheartening to have the already low supply of pencils, crayons, paper and so on, further depleted by uninvited weekend visitors (who, often as not, are pupils from the school).

Granby Street school is fortunate in having a playing field. Most Toxteth schools have very little or no green areas to play on. But the field has its drawbacks. People walk their dogs there, with the inevitable consequences. Most dogs simply run wild there, and don't observe school timetables, thus causing havoc during games periods. Motorbikes have driven across the field during games lessons. And inevitably, the area is littered with all kinds of rubbish, especially broken glass, which remains well hidden in the grass.

Despite the uphill struggles, there is much to be praised in Toxteth schools. On primary school outings, the overwhelming experience of teachers from all over the city is that the pupils from the inner-city schools are among the best behaved. (I've heard it suggested that this may be because they have so little self-assurance or confidence that they are overawed by outings and visits.) Nevertheless, they are appreciative of days out or theatre visits, and they often do well at inter-school art or sports competitions.

Yet I keep wondering what it's all ultimately for. The little ones begin so timidly, and are loved and cajoled into enjoying school. (And that includes even those wild newcomers who haven't experienced any discipline at home, and need to be tamed to conform to a socially acceptable behavioural norm.) And most continue to enjoy it overall until they are a year or two into secondary school. And then it takes exceptional, dedicated, even inspired teaching to persuade most children I meet round here that it is worth putting in any effort.

Staff at one primary school told me of three lads who had been tough pupils, but had attended school regularly, and responded reasonably well. Within weeks of starting secondary school, they were all expelled.

Why? I asked. They couldn't be sure. But it had something to do with the day-in, day-out commitment of a primary school teacher who does everything with one particular class, taking time and effort to build up a relationship with each pupil, and the much bigger, less personal atmosphere of the secondary school system, where teachers don't have the time to build those points of contact with individual pupils. They may not even see it as their job; their job is to teach French or chemistry, and if a pupil refuses persistently to respond positively then he or she is not a useful or helpful person to have in your classroom.

What are we educating our children for? Volumes of books have addressed themselves to this question, and I don't propose to set about answering it; just asking it. In one way, we're fortunate. Thomas and Alexis don't have any particular learning difficulties, they have an above-average chance of getting into the desirable Church of England secondary school, we have the qualifications to assist their education, we can generally find money for trips or equipment, and their long-term chances of further education are (as things stand) high.

That's because we conform, by accident as much as by design, to the system of which education is a part. We understand the system; we have the power to 'work' it if we choose. At least we can use the system to the boys' best advantage, having similarly used it to our own advantage.

But when I look at many of my friends and neighbours, I see a different picture. A parent may well say, 'I want Jo to have all the advantages I never had.' A worthy sentiment, no doubt, but no longer realistic.

The fact is, the parents of this generation of school children, the older ones at least, probably had more advantages than their children will. Many would have been able to find jobs when they left school, even if they haven't got one now. With unemployment averaging eighty per cent among white, and ninety per cent among black school leavers in this particular area, the idea of getting a job is as much a fantasy as their scoring a goal at Anfield.

People in Toxteth were asked about their hopes and fears as citizens of Liverpool in the church survey I mentioned at the beginning of the last chapter. These were the sort of answers they gave for their hopes:

to manage to get a job . . .
that my son would be given an adequate chance to grow up and be employed and be happy . . .
I hope I don't get mugged and raped when I'm older . . .
I haven't any . . .

And their fears:

that Liverpool will become a ghost town and a complete no-go area . . .
I'm afraid to out, frightened of being mugged and broken into . . .
staying unemployed for the rest of my life . . .
rioting because of unemployment and lack of play-space . . .
being a dole-ite . . .

How can teachers educate children in their care to face those issues? What use is arithmetic to someone who is terrified of being raped, or geography to someone afraid of leaving the house?

What our children are being taught ought to be frequently reviewed and re-evaluated. Teachers have to build on the existing foundations within each child, which may be very shaky, or have serious flaws in them.

Stephen experienced an unexpected jolt when taking RE lessons in primary school. Each year, the point would be reached in the syllabus where the parables of Jesus demonstrate the father-love of God (such as the story of the prodigal son). And each year, the response of many of the young children in his class would be blank incomprehension or rejection. Well over half the children in one class he taught either had no father at home, or had a succession of 'uncles'; or wished fervently that the bully who was their father, wasn't.

He ceased using the Lord's Prayer in assemblies, because to see that their twisted concept of fatherhood was personified in God, added insult to their injury.

Every single school day in Toxteth, there are dozens of children to be seen about the place who, for one reason or another, haven't gone to school. Illness is rarely the reason.

It may be that there is a sick relative at home who needs someone to run messages. It may be that someone has to mind the baby. It may (even in the 1980s) be that the child lacks shoes, or a coat, or clean underwear. But frequently it's because school is a take-it-or-leave-it affair, having very little to do with the real business of life, attended only when the boredom of the street corner becomes unbearable.

9

Poverty isn't Romantic

'Forests, leafy glens, running streams and sandy coves . . . '
A description of Toxteth Park, once the royal park of King
John, established in 1207.

Here is a more contemporary description, the first impressions of a self-confessed 'middle-class southerner', who came to live in Toxteth some years ago.

'Is that mist or smog?'
'Smog.' Dirty, dust, litter, dog-mess,
broken glass, graffiti, stray dogs –
That's the pavement. The back alley is worse.
A rat.
Close-packed houses, no gardens, derelict houses.
Blocks of flats three or four high with stinking dirty
staircases, graffiti-covered walls; some boarded up with
corrugated iron.
Some with carpets and washing hanging over balconies
on which dogs are tied up.
Men on street corners, standing outside the betting shop,
play football with their children.
Men all day.

Impressions that stay with you. And it's the image that I want to impress on people. There are many clean, neat, attractive homes and many well-adjusted, happy, healthy residents. They don't need me to tell their story, although it's a matter of pride to them that the rest of the world recognises that not everyone in Toxteth is inadequate or unemployed or discontented.

Lots of people in Liverpool feel the same way. 'We're *not* all poor and unemployed. We're just ordinary people leading ordinary lives,' I heard a young Liverpudlian protest over the radio.

I understand that reaction, but I also fear that this attitude ('I don't want to hear about the bad side of things all the time') is a very small step away from saying, 'It's nothing to do with me anyway,' or, 'If I pretend it isn't there, maybe it will all just go away.'

It won't. Sooner or later we are going to have to challenge the foundations of our present economic and political assumptions, and see whether a whole new social, economic and political restructuring is necessary to face the widening gap between the haves and the have-nots. The nature and degree of the problems faced by so many calls for salvation in its broadest sense, a salvation which affects the whole structure of families, communities, and the broader society, as well as each individual within those groups.

What is this salvation? It begins at the cross of Jesus, where he took our infirmities, our sorrows, our transgressions and our iniquities; and through which he gives us peace instead of the punishment we deserve; where we receive healing through his wounds.

And then it spills out to affect, ultimately, all of God's creation, which 'itself will be liberated from its bondage to decay and brought into the glorious freedom of the children of God' (Romans 8.21).

Salvation isn't isolated within an individual's experience. It has of necessity to be personally experienced, but each individual is also called to be part of the great communion of God's people, stretching from the dawn of time, on through today, and beyond into a glorious eternity. And our temporal lives are lived out on the same earth which God spoke into being, which he pronounced to be very good and which he set on its foundations so that it can never be moved.

Salvation is an all-embracing experience, not an exclusively spiritual one. God 'richly provides us with everything for our enjoyment' (1 Timothy 6.17), not necessarily wealth and riches, but rather benefits that will enrich our whole lives, thus enabling us to experience 'fulness of joy' in his presence. Before my husband Stephen became a Christian, he was sure that there was a God, because of the glory and wonder of creation. Becoming a Christian meant that he now knew who to thank for that creation.

Morris Maddocks, in his book *Journey to Wholeness*, suggests that there are four areas of relationship that are essential to our wholeness and health. The first two are drawn directly from the two great Deuteronomic laws, and the others are implicit in those laws and in the creation order. They are as follows: I need to have a healthy relationship with God, with my neighbour, with myself, and with the soil.

I remember hearing Morris Maddocks discuss these four essential ingredients for health at a conference on healing. I instinctively felt that he was right, but part of me cried out in a kind of silent rage, because I saw that people in and around Granby, and much of Toxteth, and in inner cities the world over, will never achieve even seventy-five per cent of wholeness, because we've lost contact with the soil, with God's earth, with his creation.

I realise that many others, such as those who live in luxury city-centre apartments, for example, suffer the same deprivation. They, however, had the privilege of choice. The residents of Granby (and inner cities and slum-dwelling all over the world) are not given that privilege.

There is a rather schmaltzy illustration of 'a recipe for happiness' which goes something like this: 'Take a large field, sprinkle liberally with wild flowers and scatter a few trees. Add six or seven golden children of various types and ages, and one soppy dog. Stir well and bake under a hot sun.' Behind the schmalz there is sense of the God-given healthiness and *shalom* that all parents want their children to enjoy; and that most adults yearn for too, although we cannot always define that longing.

When we go away from Liverpool in the summer, I get a shock when I see how pale our boys look in comparison to the children we meet in Devon, Yorkshire, Surrey or Wales.

Streets and backyards are no substitutes for gardens and fields, or the beach. However far inland you are in the UK, it only takes a few hours to reach the coast. Even so, plenty of children get no more than one day of sea air a year – and many don't get that. A walk on a wet day simply doesn't have the same appeal in grey city streets as in a green suburb, or out in the country, or along a windy beach.

We're out of touch with 'the soil'. New houses have been built around this area during the last few years – attractive, if small, houses, with faces and character. Not the chimney-less, colourless boxes of past decades; at least that lesson has been learnt to some extent.

It's apparent to anyone walking around the new streets that something is not quite right about them. Many are well decorated, with pretty curtains at the little windows; they look cosy and homely. The contrast is in front of the house: in the garden. These new houses have little gardens, front and back. Yet only about half of them are cultivated.

Many are overgrown; a few are rubbish tips. One has plastic flowers in it. People have lost touch with the earth they were created for and from.

Talk to any gardener of the benefits of time spent in caring for plants, in just digging a patch of ground over, and it's obvious that the rewards outweigh the energy expended, or the aching back and blistered hands.

It seems a double tragedy that people who have been deprived of contact with the soil for much of their lives don't know what to do with it when they have it. Many have (not by choice) time to spend on their gardens, but they don't know how to, or simply don't want to.

Environment, health and housing issues loom large in discussions about the inner city, but I wonder how often the use of gardens is considered, or the importance of people's relationship with the land. To be at odds with, or uninterested in the very earth itself seems to me to be an indicator of a kind of sickness, a blindness which affects bodies, minds and spirits.

I didn't need the *Faith in the City* report, or the innumerable sociological studies on the market to tell me that poverty, poor housing and long-term unemployment can lead to low self-esteem and poorer health. I just walk around with my eyes open, and know how to add two and two together.

However, I do realise that if anything is to be done to break this cycle at a local, national or international level, studies have to be done, research carried out, and reports have to be made to the bodies with the power, the influence and the resources to effect change.

The inner cities are the places where industry, and in particular manual work, has declined. Many manual workers live in the inner cities. More and more people are looking for fewer and fewer jobs. Sooner or later most give up trying to find paid work.

Society, including schools, the Church and the Government, communicates the message that to work for a living is the norm. Not many want to be deviants, yet millions have been forced to be. And the message continues, 'What you do is what you are.'

I've faced conflict over this issue. Since we married, I've had only occasional paid employment, by choice. I've not needed to work to supplement our income. We chose to live on Stephen's income; we had the added security of knowing that we could rely on it for the foreseeable future.

I usually find that the first question I'm asked when I meet someone new (at least, outside Toxteth) is, 'What do you do?' And when I've mumbled something about being at home, it's: 'Well, what did you do *before* you had the children?' I dread this moment. Unless we can change the course of the conversation, it's about to die – I can't identify myself by what I do, but how else can I justify my existence? Sometimes I end up feeling foolish, inadequate, and a non-contributor to society. As Stephen has tried to reassure me, it's the initial question that is misplaced.

Among the unwaged, some become depressed, some attempt suicide. Depression affects general health. A person may have less incentive to look after himself, becoming more susceptible to illness, and finding he has fewer reserves to fight it off. And it affects his wife and children; the strain on him is carried by them all, falling particularly heavily on the wife, who may be working, or looking for work herself, as well as trying to hold the family together and care for a demoralised husband.

The less money you have, the less choice you have over housing. Many homes still lack basic amenities, or are in desperate need of repair. And many are, simply, quite depressing. Those in greatest need get the 'hard-to-let' properties, which are, by definition, pretty hard to live in too. Put a depressed person into a depressing environment . . .

Surely, people say, tenants can do something to cheer their homes up? Some potted plants perhaps; a new coat of paint?

Let's assume the best. Assume that there isn't any damp, or not much anyway, that the plasterwork hasn't many cracks or holes, that there is a lavatory seat, that the electricity hasn't been cut off, that the paper isn't hanging off the wall, that the front door has a lock on it, that stray cats or dogs (or rats) haven't got inside, that the walls aren't sprayed with graffiti, that it doesn't smell like a urinal – to name but a few of the problems tenants may have to face.

This is what happened to Nora. She had had a very good,

secure job for many years since she'd been widowed. She was a very attractive woman in her forties. Then she became ill, and had to take time off work. She found it hard to manage in her flat, and became anxious about being stuck up there all alone, and asked to be rehoused in a new, more secure flat.

Her ill-health, coupled with the uncertainty of her future brought on a mental breakdown, and she spent some time in hospital. When she came out, her new flat was ready and she moved in.

But things didn't improve. Without her familiar surroundings and neighbours, she became depressed. Would she be able to return to work? Would her health improve? Unable to cope, she let everything go. Her appearance was unkempt, and she neglected her personal hygiene. The flat became filthy.

Friends offered to organise a work party to come in and spring-clean the place. Someone offered to do her hair, someone else to do some washing. Such was her state that for many months she refused any offers of help. She was so depressed, she 'couldn't be bothered' with any of it.

Eventually, however, a small miracle occurred. Nora got a neighbour to cut her hair, and asked a friend to accompany her to a local dress shop. She had all her old furniture taken away to a tip, and bought new carpets, curtains, furniture, and paint for the walls. She even filled the rooms with flowers.

I learnt four lessons from Nora's experience. The first one was how very easy it is to keep on sliding down once you've taken one step on to the path of deprivation. It was health that Nora was deprived of initially, but that was enough.

The second lesson was how hard it is to help someone up from the bottom. It's easiest if you go and stand next to them and point the way out to them. But it may seem too hard, too far, too much – and the resources of aid may seem too inadequate.

Next, Nora had one great advantage. She actually had money – money she'd saved before her illness, and benefit accrued during her illness. So it was financially possible for her to make all those radical changes to herself and her flat that proved to be such a boost to her self-confidence and morale.

Finally, she had the prayers and practical support of a church. God didn't want to see her destroying herself any more than her friends did.

So Nora had material and spiritual resources at her disposal, and her story has a happy ending. The majority of poor people, however, have no direct access to either – and they need both to conquer the despair that is the bread and butter of their lives.

Groups are commissioned, and campaigns organised to alleviate the problems; yet there is an increasing number of people who are trapped by unemployment, bad housing, poor health and so on. Three out of ten people in the UK live on or below the poverty line, while the rich and comfortably off continue to get richer, aided by welfare and tax policies.

Single people have no legal right to be housed; they often have to live in commercial hostels, where the rent is higher than the benefit to which they are entitled. Those under the age of twenty-six are likely to be made to move on every few weeks, so they find themselves without a permanent home, and their job prospects become even more remote.

The alternative of staying at home with parents or in-laws is far from ideal. Being an extended family by choice is very different from having that life-style forced upon you. The pressures on marriages in such an environment are often too great. The idea of 'setting up home' is no more than a romantic dream for many young couples.

Ethnic minorities experience racism when they are looking for housing, sometimes quite openly. A report in 1984 showed that, although ninety-one per cent of the population said that they thought racial prejudice was wrong, thirty-three per cent admitted that they were prejudiced, and forty per cent considered that the problem was increasing. On a television documentary, it was claimed that 'white people refuse to accept that racism exists in such a profound way as it does'. So ethnic minorities may be further disadvantaged by prejudice, and the majority of people, not recognising the degree to which it exists, take no steps towards its eradication.

It is also among ethnic minorities that problems occur in health care. Language barriers can be very distressing and frustrating. Many Asian women are very intimidated by the system.

The Liverpool 8 Neighbourhood Health Project, set up in 1984, has tried to alleviate this problem, by providing assistance for Asian women in communicating with doctors, and ensuring that they see women doctors. Unhappily, the facility has hardly been used. Yet the need is there.

Some people are just too scared to go to see a doctor. There is evidence to show that, although people in Urban Priority Areas are less healthy and less well provided for than their more prosperous neighbours, it tends to be the latter group who are reached by the various policies and projects promoting health care, such as better diet and advice about smoking, heart disease, alcohol consumption and so on.

Faith in our City, a response by a Merseyside group to Part III of the *Faith in the City* report, considers that 'The medical practice in Urban Areas (as elsewhere) requires humility, honesty, courtesy and the demystification, not the deification, of medicine.' It further recommended that chaplains should be linked with general practices, health centres and community clinics. It discussed the need to enable people to accept and understand suffering, and for churches to enable services such as bereavement counselling.

There is much to be encouraged by in such suggestions,

and much to work towards. A wholistic (as Morris Maddocks prefers to spell it) approach to health and medicine is a biblical norm. Christians need to recognise and affirm this.

Nevertheless, the problem remains of putting people in touch with practitioners in the first place. The Neighbourhood Health Project has offered various courses and information on a large range of perceived needs, such as anxiety and depression, sickle cell anaemia, cot death, issues relating to old age, women's health, men and sex, and to hyperactivity in children.

They advertise in public places (like libraries), in schools, making use of Parent Centres, and on the streets, setting up a stall for a day. And now (at the time of writing) they face the imminent withdrawal of their funding, and everything that they have taken time to build up will be lost.

Jim Wallis is an American social activist and writer on social issues like urban deprivation who has set up a special community as part of his work for the dispossessed and the marginalised. In an interview for the publication *City Cries*, he said, 'I'm not trying to romanticise the poor; I've lived too long in a poor neighbourhood to be romantic about poverty or the poor. Jesus is present among the poor, not because they are more noble, but because they are more vulnerable.' (Like the man living in a squalid flat a few hundred yards from here who has fixed iron railings inside his front door because he is afraid of intruders.)

The church is being exhorted from many sides once again to speak out with a prophetic voice to the nation. I guess most of us would rather keep nice and quiet, or at most, to encourage someone else to open his or her mouth. But we can no longer afford to remain silent. Those of us not directly affected by society's injustices, are none the less involved and implicated, however distasteful that seems to us.

We have power to effect change. We have spiritual power: 'The weapons we fight with are not the weapons of the world.

On the contrary, they have divine power to demolish strong-holds' (2 Corinthians 10.4). Prayer is not just the last resort, it should be the beginning and the middle too.

We can try to educate ourselves, to be more aware of how different sections of our society live. Many Christian books have been written on this and related issues.

How about a visit to your nearest inner city? Not a coach trip with cameras and flasks of coffee; maybe just you and a friend, and God, to open your hearts as well as your eyes and minds.

Thus equipped with a better understanding of the nature of some of the problems, we can think about what economic and political changes need to be made, and put pressure on those who have the power to effect change locally and nationally. After all, they are there to represent us.

To come full-circle, we need finally to open our hearts to allow God's light to shine on our prejudices tucked away in dusty corners, and to look again at the choices we have made, the things (or people) we are afraid of, our dreams for the future. We need to recognise the pressing need for the whole church to cry out together to God for forgiveness, justice and mercy.

Together we need, as Paul wrote, to 'work out [our] salvation with fear and trembling' (Philippians 2.12), to the end that all should experience God's *shalom*.

And let us learn lessons in grace and humility, recognising that what we thought were strengths may in fact be weak-nesses, and what we thought were weaknesses may in fact be strengths.

Jim Wallis, in the same interview mentioned earlier, said:

Spiritually, I am impressed by the resilience of poor peo-ple, how they survive in the face of overwhelming odds. That is something most middle-class people just don't have. The middle-class think the problem is that the poor people don't have the resources to survive: 'If they did, they'd be more like me.' Now I don't know many middle-class people who have the kind of resourcefulness to survive nearly as well as those families survive, amidst difficulties most middle-class people could never imagine.

10

Behind Church Doors

During the nine days between the glazing of the windows of St Nathaniel's church, Windsor, Liverpool, and its consecration, no less than seventy-six panes of glass were broken. That was in 1870. Just over a hundred years later, Stephen and I joined that church. We recall an afternoon when the vicar had to dodge the rebounding half-brick *he* had thrown at the newly-installed fibre-glass brick- and bullet-proof windows. The building contractor had recommended this test of their effectiveness.

In the five years we were there, Stephen and I became engaged, finished college, married, began work, had our first baby and took part in various church activities, including cleaning, catering, flower arranging, Sunday school teaching, singing in the choir and, on my part, being secretary to the PCC and even, briefly, as a last and desperate measure on the part of the church, playing the organ.

I had been on an Easter retreat during the year before that action-packed five-year period began. I'd rather lost my way spiritually, but somehow, without any great drama, God turned me round that week, and I knew it was his way I had to follow.

Stephen (though I didn't know it at the time) became aware of a perceptible change in me, and he began his own investigations into Christianity. On the first Sunday that Advent, he took communion at the Anglican cathedral, and counts his conversion from that day.

The Family Eucharist service at the cathedral was relaxed and friendly, but although we both attended for a while, we knew that we would rather belong to a local parish church. And so, at the recommendation of members of the university Christian Union, we found our way to St Nathaniel's, in the part of Toxteth known as Windsor.

It was a low conservative evangelical church, although we weren't particularly conscious of such labels and their significance at the time. It was a friendly church, as I have since discovered most Toxteth churches to be, almost without exception. Stephen began teaching at the church primary school.

We had to find somewhere to live too, now that we were leaving our student flats and setting up home together. We wanted to live as near as possible to the place where we worshipped. This was complicated by the entire parish being made up of corporation property. We chose to look for a privately owned place to rent, rather than be added to the long lists of people waiting for council homes. Perhaps we felt that we were able to make a choice here that many were unable to make, corporation homes being their only option.

And so we found our flat, acquired our furnishings from the famous Paddy's Market, and became very serious about the business of being married. (Perhaps not quite serious enough, because older members of the congregation always referred to us and our contemporaries as 'The Students'.)

We read the new books on the market about Christian marriages. I seem to recall that I was exhorted, as a good wife, to be perfumed and manicured and unflustered when my husband returned from his hard day's labour, and to save all my problems and worries, and the bills, until after he was relaxed and fed. And Stephen was encouraged to bring me flowers and chocolates, and sit me on his knee, and dry the dishes for me. (Not all at the same time.)

Perhaps my memory is a little clouded with a certain cynicism, but I now abhor the role-stereotyping, the assumed middle-classness and affluence typical of many of those books, superficially so inappropriate to many of the marriages round about here; although, buried beneath the frippery and foolishness were, perhaps, some unchanging biblical truths. (Not that I refuse flowers and chocolates . . .)

That's how we came to live in Granby. It was as near to St Nathaniel's parish as we could make it. It was tough, but we had the energy and enthusiasm for a challenge. And of course, I didn't expect us to be there for long. I still had an escape route: to York, where I'd grown up, and where my father still lived. There we could go and be part of St Michael-le-Belfrey, rejoicing in the worship and absorbing David Watson's teaching. It was as if I took a deep breath and plunged down under the waters of Liverpool just as long as I could bear it, finally rushing up again for the air that was York.

When there, I would pluck up courage to ask for prayer for St Nathaniel's parish, and Stephen's school. But it was before the infamous events of the summer of 1981, and no one had really heard of Liverpool 8; and the slums and deprived areas of Liverpool which probably sprang to the prayers' minds couldn't stir the imagination to the same degree of urgency that a visit to the place itself might have done. And even then, it takes more than a visit just to begin to understand the sheer wearing-down-ness of inner-city existence. But I was grateful for the concern shown and the prayers prayed.

David Watson did in fact once preach at St Nathaniel's. Afterwards he remarked that it was the only time he'd preached while stones and bricks were being hurled at the church windows. We wryly gauged our spiritual temperature by the degree of spiritual opposition evidenced by the varying amounts of stones thrown at the windows. The heavier the barrage, the more we considered that God was active in the church. It was certainly tangible spiritual warfare.

When, during a summer mission in 1973, workers (including Stephen) were physically attacked in the church hall by a gang led by a practising Satanist, it was not because of any physical counter-attack that they left, but because the Christians began proclaiming aloud the name of Jesus, and the gang simply turned on their heels and fled. One of them was later arrested, tried and imprisoned for grievous bodily harm.

Yet with hindsight, I believe that at that point many in the church felt that they had got their fingers burnt and didn't like it. We were handling dynamite, it scared us, and we backed off.

It wasn't a comfortable church to be part of. You didn't go there to show off your hat. At every service we had 'bouncers' – church wardens and other hefty men – on duty at the doors. Frequently we left the building in a large group rather than in ones or twos – we feared, not without reason, some kind of aggression from the local gangs of teenagers (and their younger brothers and sisters), with whom we had an uneasy relationship. They were great kids, but just a little volatile and unpredictable. They burned our church hall down one day. Children of all ages frequently interrupted our services in a variety of loud and disruptive ways (hence the bouncers). We tried hard to forge friendships with them and their families, with varying degrees of success.

It had always been a tough parish. In the words of the first vicar, Canon Richard Hobson, 'Its area was, socially and morally, the lowest in the south-east portion of Liverpool.' Not a lot has changed. Old housing, with areas such as 'the little hell', has been replaced with new, which in turn has become run-down or derelict. Many advertisements for labourers in those nineteenth-century days used to warn, 'Windsor men need not apply.' It would seem that the same slogan is stamped invisibly across similar advertisements today.

St Nathaniel's has always been distinctly Protestant in its outlook. As with the first vicar, the incumbent during our involvement with the church felt very strongly that there was absolutely no room in a Christian church for any 'Romanism'. Both vicars were supporters of the Orange Lodge, which has considerable strength in parts of Liverpool. For many Liverpudlians you are distinguished by two criteria: whether you support Liverpool or Everton; and whether you are Catholic or Protestant.

All bound up in our Christian experience was what was then generally referred to as the charismatic movement. It was part and parcel of what we still consider to be the fundamentals of our faith. But because Roman Catholics were also involved, our vicar (understandably from his point of view) could not accept this as being from God.

What we were learning – about love and its expression, about the Body of Christ and commitment – through the charismatic movement, we endeavoured to practise, along with others (notably among 'The Students'). But others resisted strongly, and tensions and misunderstandings sprang up.

The crunch came for us when Stephen was training as a lay reader, and beginning to preach regularly, and found, to his consternation, that the thrusts of his preaching and our vicar's were in danger of coming into opposition.

On many occasions they would sit down together and thrash out the issues involved, and pray for a solution. In the end, they agreed lovingly to differ, and our vicar recommended St Gabriel's church to us, on the west side of Toxteth, where our spiritual priorities would accord with those of the leaders there, and he graciously contacted them on our behalf.

I include this rather unhappy episode because it has a twofold significance. The first is personal: it explains how we came to be members of a church which is in a very different part of Toxteth (albeit only a twenty-minute walk away) from where we live.

Secondly, it has been one of the most sobering experiences of my life to watch the once-thriving St Nathaniel's become a redundant, derelict shell, as it was by the time of the 1981 riots which raged within a few yards of the empty building.

It's hard to know what interpretation to put on all this. I believe that St Nathaniel's radically changed direction after the experiences of the 1973 summer mission, and became effectively entrenched in things we understood and knew we could handle. Protestantism became, to some, at least, disproportionally important, and we seemed to back-pedal into form and tradition. It was as if God opened a new door for us, and we looked in, and shook our heads, and walked the other way, back to familiar territory. Only we left God on the other side of the door.

Others, perhaps, may interpret the events differently. Needless to say, it hurt all of us deeply, especially those who couldn't even grasp the concept of what was happening, let alone come to their own conclusions about it. But I remember my time there with lots of love and gratitude.

So began a new era for us, and by now Thomas was all of two months old. A sense of family has always been a feature of St Gabriel's – there was always someone, somewhere, who was pregnant. A few weeks after our arrival, Stephen read a lesson in the Christmas carol service with Thomas strapped on to his front in a baby sling. A diocesan survey one year came up with the startling fact that the average age of the entire congregation was eight!

Families have to live together and learn to love each other with all the manifold attendant problems . . . and that's what St Gabriel's, old and young, married and single, was learning. I think that all of us involved in that process will be eternally grateful for the experience, and friendships forged then have a unique quality. The friendliness of St Gabriel's has been commented on time and again, and that is significant, because that sets the atmosphere for anyone coming into the church, either regularly or as a visitor or newcomer.

What of other local Christians? Where else do people round here worship? In 1982, ECUM (The Evangelical Coalition for Urban Mission) commissioned a report of a research study carried out by Michael LeRoy, entitled *Riots in Liverpool 8: Some Christian Responses*. It is a valuable account and analysis of the events surrounding that traumatic episode in our local history.

According to the report, there are forty churches of one kind or another in the study area – which extends well beyond the boundary of Granby. This includes the Christian Scientist church, and the two Nigerian sects: the Church of the Lord Aladura, and The Brothers of the Cross and the Star. There is also a Jehovah's Witness Kingdom Hall.

Within the Granby triangle, there is a Roman Catholic church, a Methodist church, Emmanuel Church (originally a Holiness church), and an Anglo-Catholic church which also provides a meeting-place for a Nigerian Christian congregation. More or less next door is a synagogue, and nearby is a mosque. Just beyond the border of the triangle is an evangelical Anglican church, a Greek Orthodox church, and a small Baptist church. Plenty of variety available to anyone wanting to worship.

During our time here, the character of some of the churches has changed. Emmanuel Holiness Church, for example, is known simply as Emmanuel Church, since Ewen Gillespy began to pastor it. Ewen has lived here with his family a few years longer than us, working until quite recently as a youth worker in the Methodist Centre.

The church is situated almost opposite their home. Those who attended were mainly elderly people, commuting from as far away as the Wirral. Now, albeit very slowly, local people are beginning to come to the church.

It's all too easy to criticise the commuters. LeRoy comments, 'Many . . . commute back to their old church for reasons not dissimilar to those who commute back to their old pub. They return to a group with which they feel familiar, and to keep in touch with their friends and relatives, perhaps also because the churches in their new area exude a different class culture.'

Most Toxteth churches probably have several commuters among their members, by no means all of whom are elderly. Many would object to LeRoy's assessment of their motivation.

So, why do people commute? Initially, a choice is made; either to move out to a suburban environment or, for some, to come in to worship in an inner-city church; a significant shift of emphasis. The latter group may wish to identify with their inner-city sisters and brothers, while some of the former group may be seen as no longer wanting to identify with them.

Generally, church commuters are those who have moved out. Some had no choice; they were rehoused. And many of them would have preferred to stay where their roots are. (Granby, alas, doesn't always prompt such loyal feelings. The rest of Toxteth disowns it. I happened to mention to members of a church just beyond the Granby border that several houses in Granby were for sale. 'You wouldn't see me dead there,' one man said, and the others nodded their agreement. They were not joking.)

Some move out to the inner or outer suburbs for the sake of their children's education, or to improve their job prospects . . . (Remember, 'Windsor men need not apply.')

Others live on the fringes of the inner city. There is a road sign framed by the lush greenery of Sefton Park announcing entry into Toxteth. (Not all of Toxteth is broken glass and graffiti. There are some salubrious bits. But all it amounts to really is that the postcode is wrong.) It's a wise choice for those wishing to be identified with the inner city, but not sure about leaping in up to their necks.

So, whether from inside or outside, Sunday by Sunday Christians meet in the various churches. Many would describe themselves as committed to their church and, thereby, to the community. But what is the nature, or basis of that commitment? The staff of the local Health Centre are very committed. Teaching staff at the local schools are committed. Local councillors, youth and community workers are committed. It is good that church members also are committed to want to bring about change in the community – but what kind of change? Much of this work is carried out equally well by many other religious, political or humanist groups.

There has to be something more, something distinctively unique on offer for the church to be able to claim that it is different from any other agency, organisation or religion. Sometimes Christians and churches spend too much time trying to blend into their surroundings, adapting *so* well that they lose their saltiness and fail to stand out as beacons of light.

Our tragedy is that so many Toxteth churches disagree – or think that they do – on the fundamentals of faith, and disagree again on the outworking of those fundamentals.

In LeRoy's view, 'inter-church life in Toxteth does not seem particularly vigorous. Between a few churches there has been a sharing of facilities and exchange of pulpits, but most pursue their own course with little apparent sense that they travel the same ocean.'

The Toxteth Evangelical Association draws together the leaders of a dozen or so churches; and various annual events (such as a Good Friday evening youth rally) are organised. But again, other churches are excluded, albeit by their own choice. And the Anglican Church is still viewed with suspicion by many independent evangelical churches.

'I didn't know there were any "born-again" Church of England churches,' someone said to me. A questionable – and loaded – way of putting it, but I appreciated what she was driving at. I'm pretty sure she would find quite a few Toxteth Anglican churches would fit her definition of 'born-again', being by no means bound by the liturgical tradition and upper-middle-classness that the media portrays the Anglican Church as having. That isn't to say that there is no liturgy, or that it is always culturally appropriate, or that there is no longer any middle-class orientation. But at least there is an increased awareness of the need to challenge some of the long-held beliefs and traditions which have out-worked their usefulness, and to adopt a 'back to basics' approach.

Again, writes LeRoy, 'the predominant impression of the non-Anglican churches is of relatively small, inward-looking congregations. Many of these are long-established and have an elderly membership. Their style is dated. A member commented about his own church, "It's not related to life any more." '

What's the solution? Here are churches which were established when this was a completely different community – the location hasn't changed, but just about everything else seems to have done. Larger national churches have greater resources to face this upheaval and change and have the potential to adapt as necessary, but it's not so easy for the smaller churches, especially where the congregation is made up of faithful elderly people. It's one thing to change course when you're young, healthy, able to face a challenge, but it is expecting a great deal more of a group of elderly people who, apart from all these considerations, may indeed have their personal histories bound up in their church.

I'm not familiar with all of Toxteth's churches; indeed, until reading LeRoy's report, I didn't know some of them existed. Of those I have visited, I've always found the atmosphere friendly and welcoming. But even after a lifetime of learning to deal with different styles of worship (Holy Communion, Mass, the Eucharist, the Lord's Supper, an Agape Feast, to name a few), I still make mistakes in unfamiliar territory. So it's easy to appreciate why it takes a fair bit of courage for someone unused to church to step over the threshold. Their heads are probably stuffed with images of church from TV comedy shows or shock horror stories of vicars and choirmasters from the popular newspapers.

You feel very intimidated if a pile of books is thrust into your arms when you're not very good at reading. And what about the collection? What if you've forgotten it – or you've only got a fiver on you – do you pretend to put something in the bag as it's passed round? Or what if no one told you to put something in the box by the door, and now the contents are being presented to the vicar, and you feel as if you've been cheating, because it's like not paying your admission fee?

Most churchgoers probably are sensitive to such details around here, and newcomers are given genuine welcomes and assistance in finding places and following the order of things. And then newcomers soon feel free to come along when they can (which may not be until after the service has begun), and free to leave to go to the toilet during the prayers if they need to, or to yawn copiously in the sermon if they need to – in other words, they feel free to be themselves.

We all tend to shout at foreigners until someone points out to us that because they don't understand us so well, it doesn't follow that they are therefore deaf. But what happens when we talk with someone less articulate than ourselves? We modify and adapt what we're saying to a child to a level suitable for his or her age. Unfortunately, some of us address less articulate adults with the same kind of modifications that we would automatically use with a child. In other words, we talk down to them.

To my chagrin, I've noticed that I sometimes become exceptionally articulate in the company of people who aren't particularly articulate. Conversely, I can dry up in the presence of people more intellectually and academically orientated than I am. The latter situation gives me a taste of the experience of the people I'm with in the former instance. I may know that my opinions are worthy of expression, but I can't verbalise them succinctly enough. I'm afraid I won't be able to argue my case convincingly in the face of contradiction. Sometimes when I'm back at home on my own, I do a mental rerun, and this time I shine, and brush aside all objections and reason logically, and win over my audience.

But then, logical, empirical thinking is just one way of thinking, after all. Other cultures place a higher value on intuitive thought. So very many of our attitudes, our ways of thinking and reasoning, are not essentially Christian at all, but cultural. But because they're part and parcel of our history, whether family, class, national or international history, we can't make that distinction any more.

John Wimber, in his book *Power Evangelism*, points out that world-views are culturally necessary and inevitable, and by no means automatically contrary to, or opposed to, a Christian world-view. But we need to become aware of, or to reassess, our world-views, in order to reject anything that is opposed to a Christian life-style and perspective and thought process.

World-views vary considerably within a nation: city-dwellers may have a different world-view from country-dwellers; a black worker on the dole may have a different world-view from a white worker on the dole. An evangelical Christian in the Home Counties may have a different world-view from an evangelical Christian in Liverpool; one in suburban Liverpool may have a different world-view from one in inner-city Liverpool.

All this poses, for me, a quite frightening prospect of continued alienation, creating all kinds of divisions within society – North/South, black/white, waged/unwaged and so on – relating to education, politics, sex and class. Christians are as caught up in these divisions as the rest of society. There are different Christian world-views, as well as the cultural ones we throw in as well.

The inner-city church has to recognise that some of its inherited values may need to be discarded. In his book *Gutter Feelings*, Pip Wilson confronts these issues:

> It seems to me that middle-class people generally think in concepts, while working-class people think in a concrete way . . . Jim Punton . . . is quoted as saying, 'the word became flesh, but most of us Christians would be more comfortable if the *flesh* became *word*' . . . You are no less a Christian if you can't read or articulate in 'spiritual jargon'. The communication needs to be relevant to the human culture we are in. The Gospel must relate to the context we are in . . . Where injustice, oppression and poverty abound – the gospel *must* speak to all of this as well – we can't just say 'Turn to Jesus and everything will be fine.'

Pip Wilson describes how hard it has been, in his experience of working with some of the toughest teenagers in the country, to obey the command of Jesus to 'Go and make disciples'. He doesn't have a long list of teenagers converted through his ministry – not of lasting conversions, anyway. The exceptions are the ones who give their testimonies or write books – which is why they're called on to give their testimonies or write books.

Many Christians see what has become known as 'power evangelism' as a way forward which cuts through any cultural barrier. To practise power evangelism is in essence to allow God to work in power as and how he wills – in signs and wonders, in exercising the gifts of the Holy Spirit such as healing, or words of knowledge . . . The gospels and the Acts of the Apostles are full of 'power evangelism'. When the apostles Peter and John encountered the lame man begging outside the Temple in Jerusalem, they didn't give him money. Nor did they discuss with him the peace and joy that

Jesus could bring into his life. Nor did they sit down and try to understand how he was feeling about his situation. Nor did they enter into an earnest time of prayer.

'Look at us', they said, and he was all eyes and ears, expectant – but not for what he was about to receive. 'In the name of Jesus Christ of Nazareth, walk.' And Peter heaved him to his feet and it was done: total, instant healing. And then – one of my favourite verses in the Bible – he went with John and Peter into the Temple courts, 'walking and jumping, and praising God'. What sheer uninhibited glory and delight! What a sight that must have been – even if you didn't know he'd been an incurable cripple when he got up that morning. Hardly surprisingly, people were filled with wonder and amazement. And Peter seized his opportunity, and turned to address them: 'Men of Israel, why does this surprise you . . . ?'

They *were* surprised, and they were a lot more used to miracle-workers than we twentieth-century Westerners are. But that's what power evangelism is all about: letting God be God, letting him work in power – and taking the opportunity to explain to all the startled onlookers and family and friends.

For people with an orientation towards concrete thinking, this kind of evangelism is tailor-made. It isn't all talk about God; a God too often perceived as being indifferent, uncaring, middle-class and white, if he exists at all. Instead it's seeing, touching, hearing, feeling God's love (for it is his love and mercy which motivate God's intervention in this way) at first hand. Forget the sermons – they can come later. First of all come the awe and wonder, praising and rejoicing.

I'm not being entirely carried away on a cloud of wishful thinking. There are churches – and not just in the USA or among the prosperous, large charismatic British churches – where God is working in similarly exciting and dramatic ways. There's an Anglican one not so far away where men and women may pop out for a quick fag after the sermon, but will be back to pray for you, full of expectancy that God will answer their prayers, offered in broad Lancashire accents.

There are one or two churches in the heart of Toxteth where the first steps have been made in that direction; where ministers and congregations are praying for the sick and depressed, and seeing some dramatic results. The 'Smile, Jesus loves you' stickers of the 1970s seem a paltry alternative to walking up to someone and saying, 'God can heal you, and make you whole . . . Do you want him to?' Afterwards they'll probably be smiling anyway, and you won't need any stickers.

11

God Writes the Agenda

What is the church, anyway? It's the people called by God, to be, in David Watson's words, 'a special people . . . called for a relationship with Him . . . to love one another . . . to accept [and] forgive one another . . . members of the household of God travelling through the desert wastes of this world . . . until the consummation of all things in Christ'.

The church's foremost aim, he concludes, is to have hearts continuously opened to God's love, experienced through his forgiveness, thus enabling the church to express that same love and forgiveness to people of every race and background.

High or Low, evangelical, charismatic, Roman Catholic, Orthodox or Protestant, I don't think that any of the churches in Toxteth would, or could, argue that this isn't, in essence, the church's first and foremost aim. If one did, I would have grave doubts about its Christian integrity.

The ways and means of achieving this aim are bound to differ. Without it, however, the church becomes aimless and lacking in purpose. Yet in an environment with so very much need, with injustice and racism, poverty and unemployment – and so on, *ad infinitum* – crowding right up to, and even inside, the doors of the church, it is all too easy to become sidetracked from this first and foremost aim; or to be so overwhelmed by these things that we hide, as it were, in the Church, and never dare to venture beyond its walls; or to plunge into the middle of it all and get swallowed up.

What should the churches do? Become involved in local politics; develop lunch clubs for the elderly and nursery facilities for the young; create job opportunities linked with government projects; provide drop-in centres for the unwaged; run advice and legal aid centres; teach language or basic skills classes; form youth clubs, mother-and-toddlers or after-school clubs . . . to name but a few options? Each of these attempts to target a real need, and is a way of serving the community, a way of bringing people into the Church.

Let's consider the practical aspects. There are two prerequisites: plant and manpower. Most churches are blessed, or lumbered (depending on your point of view) with a building. Many of these buildings have the makings of a good plant. St Gabriel's, for example, like many nineteenth-century churches, is simply full of space; much of it is air-space between floor and ceiling. And it's never full to capacity; in fact, in the colder months we sometimes meet in the vestry.

Huge buildings . . . with huge heating bills, repair bills, general maintenance and upkeep bills, and if you bring in the surveyor, he will point out the structural damage, a faulty wiring system maybe, a leaky roof, dry rot, or subsidence. Few inner-city churches, of most denominations, including those with newer and smaller buildings, have the income to tackle such problems; in fact, many don't have the income to keep things ticking over. There just isn't enough money.

There are some lovely buildings among the local churches. St Philemon's is a modern, all-in-one plant. But they have break-ins and vandalism to face . . . frequently a church warden leaves during a service to go and chase local children off the roof.

St Bernard's, our local Catholic church, has reordered its vast interior very effectively, installing a false ceiling and erecting screens to create a smaller, more intimate worship area. But for most churches, there remains a huge gap between possible, and achievable potential. God does, without question, work miracles. Somehow though, in my experience, these particular miracles occur most frequently

113

where the congregations can give a helping hand; pull a few financial strings, maybe.

Even assuming that the plant is or could be made suitable for other uses, the other essential resource is manpower. Take St Gabriel's again. There aren't many pew-fillers. Most people have full diaries; some are, simply, too busy. Then there are people new to the church, and just to give up a Sunday morning lie-in or the preparation of the Sunday dinner (still a big local tradition) is to give up a great deal.

We had some close friends who had been through a rough time in their church. They had been lay leaders, giving and giving, until finally they were spent out. So a couple of years ago they decided to move house and change church. They joined an inner-city evangelical church, hoping to take a back seat and get their breath back. It didn't work out that way. There were too many indians and not enough chiefs, so they were welcomed enthusiastically and within weeks found themselves leading a housegroup and having several other demands made of them. It was too much. They left, and haven't attended church since.

Christians find it hard to say 'no'. Especially when saying 'no' means that something therefore won't happen at all, because there's no one else to do it, and you have to live with your conscience.

Last year the responsibility of my nursery-age Sunday school class was becoming too much. It was getting larger, but I was losing my young assistant. I could rarely get to worship with the adults in the evenings. The infant and junior class teachers were leaving. I couldn't possibly leave too – could I?

We could have found more teachers. They, too, would probably not get to an ordinary evening service. Some of them were very new Christians and had very little teaching to pass on themselves. And the teenagers were erratic in their attendance (and behaviour).

We chose not to do a botched job. We faced the alternative; let the children stay with the adults, because, after all, they're as much part of the church as the rest of us. We adults wouldn't expect our services to be led by brand-new Christians, or by people who'd outgrown or become bored with the present system, who probably aren't committed Christians anyway. So why do we inflict this kind of leadership on our children?

In that instance I said 'no', and opened the way for an alternative, instead of letting things tick over, with ill-prepared lessons and harassed Sunday school teachers. Our new system doesn't fit like a glove yet, but we're working on it.

Sometimes I feel so frustrated when I hear or read of successful churches in non inner-city areas. I suppose that, technically, Toxteth isn't really inner city, skirting, as it does, the city centre. There are several thriving city-centre churches in the UK; but the city centre and the inner city should not be confused with one another. City centres tend to buzz with activity. Inner cities are dying.

I get frustrated because those churches where things are happening as I also want to see them happen here in Toxteth, are equipped with the resources that we haven't got. First, they have the people. Not all Toxteth churches are half or three quarters empty. But within even the larger congregations, there are few indigenous (or commuting) members who are used to leadership; few from professional backgrounds used to management or organising or decision-making; few used to analysing and projecting for future planning; few who feel able or articulate enough to take on leadership roles; and there are too few to train and encourage those with the potential in any of those areas.

In prosperous churches, church collections (plus in churches where this applies, convenanting and tithing) bring in, in real, hard-cash terms, not hundreds, but thousands of pounds more per year than inner-city churches can ever raise, no matter how sacrificial the giving.

Dance, drama, music, banners, flower-arrangements – the use of these and other creative gifts enhances and enlivens worship, and can be used to great effect in street evangelism or interdenominational celebrations. But, whatever your particular talent, you have to have the gifted people to begin with, or teachers to train enthusiastic novices.

I love to make banners. I haven't made very many, and they're fairly simple – if I can paint it or glue it, so much the better. I've delved deep into my rag-bag and found lots of suitable bits of material, and haven't had to spend much money. Sometimes I've seen some lovely banners in other churches, and felt inspiration coming on . . . But my rag-bag is nearly empty, my skills are limited, and at the moment I have very little spare time. But there isn't a team of banner-makers able to do what I can't achieve at the moment.

For ten years, I've been using dance in worship. Before my first-ever attempt at this in public, I had to lock myself in my room to work it all out. Then, when I got up to perform in church, my knees were knocking and my feet were glued to the spot, so technically it was not a masterpiece. Afterwards, as I went to sit down, I was aware of one or two people with tears in their eyes – somehow it had been God's moment, and when he works, our most humble offerings take on value and dignity.

I've learnt a little technique since then, and led workshops and danced in various churches. I see it as a ministry in the same way that Paul's letters talk of teaching, preaching, healing, administration and so on as ministries – their purpose being to 'edify the church'. Dance, used under God's direction, has many roles: it can enhance worship, encourage, teach, and can have a prophetic edge to it. It is never simply performance.

Usually churches which use dance have a dance group,

116

with one or more leaders. Although I've been recognised as the 'dance leader', I've never had a regular group meeting each week. The workshops were ends in themselves, and not made up of 'dancers'. A group would come together for specific projects (although all those involved in any of those projects have since moved away from the area); but no one could afford the time to meet regularly. In the dark, no woman would be wise to make her own way to practice. Few of us owned cars; and, anyway, it isn't safe to leave un-attended cars outside our church (or many others.) Also, I'm convinced that the pressures of inner-city life have a far more wearing-down effect than many of us are consciously aware of. Already committed people often find that the additional pressures of their commitments (inadequate resources and finances and materials) further sap their energies.

I've not felt let down or handicapped by any of these absences, because I've felt that I was doing all that God required of me – unless I was foolish enough to make comparisons with non inner-city churches. He knows our limitations.

But I want to remind thriving, successful, middle-class churches of something: Rejoice in what God is doing in your church, but be aware that some of your sisters and brothers, not so very far away, love God as dearly, try to serve him as diligently, and long to express their creativity also, but remain handicapped by the resources that they don't have, yet you have in abundance. If you found yourself reduced to one guitar or an accordion to lead your singing, or didn't have the wherewithal or the skills to decorate your building with banners and flower arrangements (remember, we haven't got gardens to grow our flowers and greenery in), or couldn't use your gifts for dance and drama, what degree of emptiness would that bring into your worship?

There was a time a few years ago when there was a cluster of

St Gabriel's households in the Granby area. We began to experience what it means in David Watson's words, 'to go out in love to others, both to forgive and be forgiven'. This was a demonstration of Jesus' injunction in John 13.35, 'By this all men will know that you are my disciples, if you love one another.'

I asked Linda, a friend who moved away from our street a year ago, what impressions of Toxteth remained with her, and how they contrasted with the vastly different, pleasant, middle-class setting she and her family now found themselves in.

For her, as for me, the chief thing she had learnt, looking from a Christian perspective, was what it really meant to be loved and to love as a practical demonstration of Christian community. She recalled, for example, how when someone injured her back, friends took over in the home (without being asked). So children were taken to and from school, fed and put to bed; washing was washed and ironing ironed. I remember too, because I was the one with the bad back.

Then there was the challenge to live simply. Not so hard to do in an area where it would be ostentatious to live otherwise, because it's hard to afford to live any other way. It had practical implications for us, though. We shared resources, from babysitters to cars, washing machines to clothes. Often we took the opportunity to eat together. Many of us had keys to each others' homes, and knew we were welcome to come in uninvited. As Linda recalled, 'Walking in for a cup of tea and, while the kettle is boiling, doing the other person's washing up.'

What she finds lacking in her new community is the attitude of 'looking for ways to help each other'. Self-sufficiency is considered a virtue, so that, while people may be willing to offer help, they are far less willing to receive it, and very reluctant to ask for it. So the concept of family is lost, and with it the sharing of joys and pain, trust and honesty. 'A family', said Linda, 'doesn't need to keep account of who it helps or who has helped it. It works at helping people understand each other, in order to work together.'

I miss that time too. I miss Linda, and all the others – circumstances have broken down that mini-community. Many Christians have left Granby, or are going to have to soon, and few are moving in.

During that period, I came to believe more strongly than ever that community is probably the way forward for Christians wanting to live out their faith in the inner city.

In a society that is fragmented – where social services cannot begin to scratch the surface of needs, but where people have forgotten how to handle their own and others' crises because the social services have taken over that role, and where people have consequently had their need for one another halted – someone has to show them how to love and care again.

Individuals, singly or in small family groups, are inadequate for this task. Life and its living absorbs too much of their energies.

I envisage a group of married and single adults, with their children, living together in a large house (most inner cities have an abundance of large, derelict properties). There would be just one building to maintain, one large meal to prepare, one washing machine, one freezer . . . single people would be able to participate in the kind of family life they often feel excluded from; children would enjoy the company of a variety of adults; parents would be enabled to spend a little more time with each other. There would be plenty of problems to iron out, too; but with a creative objective, the community, in sharing the ordinariness of life together, could be a much stronger and more economical unit to reach out into the wider community.

We, and other friends, have had a variety of people living

with us over the years. We saw ourselves as extended families rather than landlords. Some of the people who stayed had problems such as depression, drug dependency, alcoholism or mental instability. Ultimately, we all found that with such people, we weren't adequate for the task. Maybe we acted as first-aid posts, but not as the agencies of healing that we wanted to be.

Why? Because we didn't have the time, space, energies or skills that our guests required, and husbands, wives and children suffered when energies were being sapped and not topped up again.

Those kind of needs simply won't go away. A lonely person may need more than an afternoon's chat. Someone just out of prison, a teenager with problems at home, a couple whose marriage is on the rocks, a young man unable to cope with the demands society makes on him, a battered wife – all, and many more, could benefit from living for a while with a group of people able, between them, to make time and space for them, able to share some of their load without being crushed by its weight.

Give people a common enemy, or a common aim, and you can draw together the most unlikely group. After the lid came off in 1981, a group of Christians from the Granby Triangle began to meet together regularly for prayer and Bible study. What an assortment we were! Black, white, Roman Catholic and fervent Protestant, waged, unwaged, student, pensioner . . . we represented a variety of differing churches, and, between us, a volatile mixture of world-views.

But we had a common aim: we hurt for our community and we sensed that God did too. So we met informally once a fortnight, and prayed and argued and talked and studied the Bible; and marvelled at what a motley crew we were, and how much we had to learn from each other.

Gradually, the need for a Christian focus in Granby Street

emerged, something that wasn't just another church – because we represented every kind of churchmanship. And so God revealed to us a vision of a shop which would be a centre for local Christians to meet, somewhere for local residents to drop by, a place to discover the love of God – and a shop.

So in the Autumn of 1984 our shop, known locally as The Christian Shop (and officially as Granby Christian Outreach) was opened. Our fortnightly meetings had exhausted themselves, but now we had a new task. We had our premises: a small shop, with a room behind and a flat above. At first we only had access to the shop. It sells stationery, books, cards and some Traidcraft items. The cards, many of which are multi-racial, are what most customers come in for. We stock Scofield Bibles for the Rastafarians. Volunteers run the shop, and each month local Christians gather to thank God for the shop, and to pray for its witness and effectiveness.

To fill in the picture a little, one of our prayers has recently been answered. The shop's trustees (who live or work locally) have been enabled to buy the whole property. To complete the idea, we're praying for someone, or more than one person, to come and live in the flat and manage the shop.

You may be familiar with Christian bookshops and gift shops. Try to erase those pictures from your mind and I'll try to create a more realistic one of The Christian Shop. Walk past the shop during fifty per cent of normal shop hours, and you'll find the shutters down. (All the shops in Toxteth have steel shutters, or, as second best, wooden shutters and bars.) Our shutters are colourful though, because a local street poet and painter has decorated them for us.

Hopefully, the shop will be open for three hours in the afternoon, and two on Thursday morning. I'm one of the Thursday morning volunteers. We decided at the beginning that there would always be two volunteers to staff the shop. Now there's usually only one each afternoon. There simply aren't enough of us to make a regular weekly commitment. If one of us can't make it one week, the shop probably doesn't open.

Above the window, 'Jesus is Lord' stands out in bold black letters in the shape of a rainbow. In the window, various small Traidcraft items, cards and religious pictures (popular for gifts), and books, are displayed. Just inside the door are the racks of cards, and there are chairs and a table and some magazines for people who want to put their feet up and have a natter, or, occasionally, a more serious conversation.

If you drop by when we're open, we'll boil the kettle and make you a cuppa. We haven't got a coffee bar. (We didn't have the resources to meet the necessary health regulations.) We'd love to extend the facilities into the back room and get it set up as a coffee lounge. We still pray to that end. Meanwhile, you're welcome to browse (we have a library section), or sit down for a chat. The volunteers usually bring a book to read, or catch up on writing letters, or knitting – sometimes business is slack. It's big news if we take five pounds in an afternoon.

I praise God for our shop. I was caught up in the initial vision for it, picturing lots of small flickering candles joining together to create one big blaze. From where I stand, it's a very small, very vulnerable light, and it's not having much impact on the darkness. Sometimes it almost goes out. But God sees it from a different angle. When I get right up next to him, and look at it, I begin to believe again that 'the light shines in the darkness, and the darkness has never put it out' (John 1.5 Good News Bible).

Michael LeRoy's report concluded that: 'Renewed churches in Liverpool 8 could be a substantial power for good. They need to be encouraged to realise the power that could be channelled through them, and to practise the whole width of Christian mission.'

Who is to encourage them? When I read the reports and testimonies of the success of other churches they often serve only to discourage me, as I realise afresh the gaping void between the potential we may have, and the realisation of that potential. How do we set our own agenda to enable us to tap what resources we have, so that we might 'practise the whole width of Christian mission'? After all, it's not as if most of us are unaware of what needs to be done, unless we stop up our ears and blindfold ourselves.

Earlier, I posed the question of what the church should do – faced as it is with such a multiplicity of social, political and economic needs, let alone spiritual ones – before considering some of the implications of limited resources. So, what *should* the Toxteth churches be doing?

The church's primary objective is to worship. It is in and through that activity, in all its richness, variety and outworking in daily living, that we recognise who God is, who we are in relation to him and to one another. So we develop a right perspective on the world.

Servants serve a master. For the church that Master is Jesus, not the plethora of needs that crowd in on all sides. The church *is* sent into the world, but it is God who sends her; she doesn't go in response to the world's call.

There is certainly much to be done in Toxteth. Christians are not the only ones who care. But they are the ones with the potential to demonstrate their care in a way that is radically different, because it is motivated by the love of God himself.

Jesus taught his disciples to love one another as he had loved them, so that others would be able to see and know that they were his disciples. I'm not sure that this is the message communicated by all the churches in Toxteth. Some may argue that caring primarily for others in our church is exclusive, but in fact it's intensely practical. God knows that it is a pretty tall order for us; I don't need to look outside the church doors on Sundays to see lots of unmet needs, lots of areas for demonstrations of love and friendship, healing and practical care. What right have we to tell the world that God loves them if we don't demonstrate that love among ourselves, however inadequately?

Perhaps some of us need to shut ourselves up together for a little while, and begin to discover again that Jesus is the Master we serve, and to learn again to hear his voice. Jesus himself only did what he saw his Father doing. He didn't heal *all* the sick, or raise *all* the dead (which would have caused not a little chaos). We need to learn to see, and hear, what it is that the Father wants us, his set-apart people in Toxteth, to do. We can be sure that he intends us to get our hands dirty.

We need not doubt that he cares for his world infinitely more than we ever can. He does not intend the pressure of the world to crush and break us. Jesus alone could carry that weight.

So God will encourage the church which makes true, living worship its priority. He will write the agenda for the practical outworking of his love for this and all other communities, if only we will listen.

12

'Let me Walk in the Fields'

If I was reading this book, I think I'd be tempted at times to put it down in frustration, and ask, 'What on earth does the author think God put her in the heart of Toxteth for if it's all such uphill work? What has been achieved? Has God been glorified as a result of her thirteen years there? The whole thing seems pretty defeatist, and the Christian life is supposed to be joyful and victorious.'

How I long to be able to write a book bursting with testimonies of lives radically changed, of broken families restored again, of tough kids turning their backs on drugs and violence and following Jesus instead, of men who spent their days hanging round the bookies now spending the time evangelising their mates. I want to write of little groups of praying Christians, expanding so that their homes overflow with new, enthusiastic Christians – a house group in each street.

If only the local churches were at least half-full of praising dynamic Christians, who in their turn go back into the community full of hope and vision and answers to at least some of its problems. If only I could walk down the street and confidently approach the sick, the depressed, the alcoholics, and say, 'In the name of Jesus, be healed.'

If only I could tell you why it *isn't* like that, although I believe that every Christian in the vicinity longs that it should be so.

This book hasn't been written to give answers. It's not a success story. As I see it, you could stack the failures sky-high, but as far as the achievements . . .

I believe in the Kingdom of God. I believe that he wants to rule and reign through his people. I believe in miracles, in healings, in God's power to change radically the direction and purpose of lives, I believe in the defeat of Satan and victory of Jesus on the cross. I believe in the reality and power of the Resurrection.

I believe . . . but if you were to ask me to show you a demonstration of those truths as they apply to Granby, I would have to come to you practically empty-handed. In real terms, I don't feel I have very much to show after thirteen years of living in Toxteth.

It's not been easy being 'ordinary' members of the community. It would have been simpler to have had a defined task or purpose; to have been youth or community workers, or ministers or pastors. It hasn't been easy belonging to a church in a different part of Toxteth, because Granby is like an island, beyond which are other countries entirely.

It's always easier to do, rather than to be. I've come to terms with our time here by recognising that we are, in Jesus' terms, salt and light. Salt and light don't do a lot, they're simply there; both are more likely to be noticed by their absence than by their activity. I assure you, it's very hard to be salt and light when what you really want is some action, some evidence of effectiveness.

Maybe, as someone from outside Toxteth suggested, the role that local Christians have played for the last couple of decades has been in many ways an underground one. Foundations have been laid on which others may come in to build. Foundations of prayer, of maybe no more than a continuing Christian presence, struggling to keep our candles alight, when winds of apathy, indifference, misunderstanding and sometimes hostility threaten to blow them out.

Paradoxically, it is a privilege to live in this community. There's not much sophistication, but plenty of vulnerability. It's not afraid to hang out its dirty linen in public. Of course, it doesn't actually have a choice – someone else (invariably the media) will do the job instead if it fails to do it itself.

Things aren't done by halves: celebration is noisy, anger is expressed rather than repressed, frustration explodes into rioting. Someone makes you mad, so you hit them. At least you know where you stand (or stood).

Father Austin Smith is a Passionist priest who has lived and worked in the Granby area for several years, and his book *Passion for the Inner City* is a very moving and challenging account of his experiences here, as well as a theological analysis of the subjects of poverty and powerlessness. He describes how, as he began his work, he found himself stopped in his 'enthustiastic apostolic tracks':

> I saw people struggling to stay alive in the midst of social neglect, poor housing, bad planning, incongruous education, political manipulation, a repulsive environment, racial discrimination and a vacuous future. But I also found hope in the centre of hopelessness . . . I was in the midst of a wounded world, yet I could still hear the heartbeat of God's creation. I was challenged to make sure that I received from this world before I could in any sense act or indeed live with relevancy.

> When I was house hunting . . . I was advised to visit an agency in the city. While I was waiting I sat next to a young mother with three small children. She was a 'one parent family' not by choice but because it had turned out that way. She had no place to go that night and only six pounds in her purse. She neither begged from me nor complained, but I thought then that it was not money or even houses which divided us, we were aliens to each other by reason of the constriction and openness of choices which we both had in life. The 'housing' condition of both of us was but a symbol of the poverty and the richness of our respective choices in life, it was the power to choose which divided us.

The fact of the matter was, there was not the slightest possibility in life that I should ever be that way, the potentiality was not there to powerlessness, never mind the actuality. I may rationalise this, but in the end I must face up to the fact that insecurity will never touch me.

I began this book by saying that it was more or less by default that we came to the inner city. There was not a 'divine calling' – at least not one that we were aware of – and I believe now that we couldn't have understood such a call if we had heard it then.

My 'passion for the inner city' has grown from within; it has not been imposed or impressed on me from an external agency giving me a task to perform here. Had God said to me, 'Go and do this and do that in Granby', I would always have been a little separate, distanced by my task, my vocation.

I do believe that Christians are called to be 'set apart', but in a different way. Jesus was wholly ordinary in his background, profession and appearance. His 'set apartness', or 'holiness', came from his unequivocal continuous obedience to his Father, God.

I had no directive to fall back on, to hide behind. I simply became a resident of Granby. Because of that, I had, in a small way, the opportunity to sense the frustration, powerlessness, helplessness of so many, and to be able to offer them almost nothing in any practical sense, having no human power or authority to alter their circumstances any more than they have themselves. It's just a matter of being there and being assailed by the shrapnel from their particular situations from time to time. That knocks away any smugness that can afflict those with some degree of power, and strips away any vestiges of superiority. 'I'm sorry, I don't know what to do either,' may be all that I can offer.

Nevertheless, as Fr Austin Smith wrote, I am also constantly aware of the multiplicity of choices that I have, and no doubt to a greater or lesser extent always will have, unlike the majority of my neighbours.

Since this book was begun, my whole future has altered. Stephen has just become an ordinand, and in a few months' time we will be leaving Granby and going to a theological college in a pleasant suburb in North London. As yet the prospect is still more a dream than a reality for me, because I've not yet visited the college and we don't know where we'll be living. But it will happen.

Then what? Will all of these years in Toxteth fade into my past? Somehow I can't countenance that alternative. In some way, the same knife of oppression that strikes down so many in our society has also forced its way into my heart, and is going to remain wedged there permanently, turning perhaps from time to time when the comforts of a different kind of life begin to submerge the alternative reality.

Potentially, we could go anywhere after Stephen's training. A small market town in the Yorkshire Dales would go down nicely . . . Instead I must face the alternative, that we *may* now have a task before us to return to the inner city, not only equipped with the skills and backed with the authority to minister in such a place, but also with hearts that have been torn apart in order to feel, in some measure, the pain of those at the bottom of the pile, and to know a little of the pain and grief that God also feels for this part of his creation.

Thomas and Alexis play 'Three Wishes': 'What would you wish for if you could have three wishes?' Of course, the first one is always 'I wish that I could have three more wishes' – so that the game can continue *ad infinitum* (or *ad nauseam*). But often they include as one of their wishes something like this: 'I wish that there would be no more war or fighting, and that everyone would share with everyone else and be nice to each other.'

If only it were that simple. In fact, it's frequently very hard to be 'nice' to people. For example, as I mentioned in an earlier chapter, a friendly smile can present enough of a challenge. We so easily misinterpret another's intentions. I can't guarantee that my smile is going to be so permeated with godly love that no man would ever again make a veiled sexual response (as happens all too often to women).

Do I have nothing to give? In a sense, the answer is yes, I have nothing. Like Fr Austin Smith, I need to make sure that I receive from this bit of the world before I presume to give anything back. The greatest gift I have to offer (I can only speak for myself) is a heart that is willing to be touched by the same things that touch God's heart, willing for mine to be broken continually in some small measure as his is broken.

That way, living my life here becomes a kind of continuing intercession. When I'm walking around, a sense of deep compassion or love or anger or sorrow may well up unbidden inside me from a source that is beyond me – because God's heart is embracing mine. That is intercession; that, I believe, is the one sure purpose I can distinguish in all the morass of my questioning and confusion (and despairing), and perhaps is all that is necessary, for now, for me to understand.

It may seem to some that my attitudes smack of arrogance and presumption. Why *should* I assume that I may have had anything to offer in the first place? Doesn't that verge on paternalism? Because I have *chosen* to live here doesn't give me any right to throw my weight about, or turn me into some kind of authority on the inner city.

I would agree. I am no authority, nor do I have any authority. The picture I paint simply shows, in a rough and approximate way, what I see. Some bits are incomplete because I don't understand what I see. Other parts may seem distorted because I'm looking at them from the wrong angle.

What really matters, however, is that all of us are in this together. Ultimately we're all naked before God. As St Paul put it 'What did we bring into the world? Nothing! What can we take out of the world? Nothing!' (1 Timothy 6.7 Good

130

News Bible). Yet we allow the things of this world to divide and separate us: class, religion, politics, background, education, social status – anyone can lengthen the list. The bigger the number of differences between you and me, the harder it is for us to find common ground. But it isn't impossible, and we must not give up trying. How much more so if we are Christians: 'You are all one in Christ Jesus' (Galatians 3.28).

High-profile campaigning on behalf of the victims of wars, famines or earthquakes that happen continents away often moves us to compassion more readily than the niggle of awareness of the downtrodden on our own doorstep. But it never has been the nature of problems to disappear because we ignore them or rationalise them.

Sometimes when I'm out of Toxteth, I have an urge (which I've so far controlled admirably) to leap up in some public place, like a library or cathedral or supermarket, and shout out: 'Do you care that Toxteth is hurting? That my neighbours want to live without violence and poverty and fear? That they want to be free to make the same kind of choices that you are free to make? What are you going to do about it?'

Should anyone come up to me afterwards (before the librarian, the Dean or the store manager) and ask me, 'Well, what do you suggest I do?', I wouldn't know how to answer. Someone living in a different inner city said, 'When people say, "What can we do to help you?" we say, "Come and live here." But that is not quite what they meant.' I don't know what other ordinary, not very influential people can do – but I'd rather that they wrestle with that dichotomy than not be confronted with it at all. To be aware has to be better than remaining unaware.

It wouldn't work for hundreds to sell up their houses and rush enthusiastically into their nearest inner city. It takes more than enthusiasm anyway. It takes commitment of years, commitment of mind, emotion, body and spirit. And you may get no thanks for it. Indeed, why should you? The majority of residents here don't get praise for living here; only criticism, rejection, rebuff.

But for those who do hurt, for those who do cry out for someone, somewhere to take notice – in other words, for those at the bottom of the pile – it does help, just a little, to know that a few 'out there' care too, maybe enough to pray, showing solidarity with their disadvantaged brothers and sisters at the foot of the cross.

Several years ago, when I was finding life here particularly hard, Stephen gave me a copy of the following poem by George MacDonald. I keep it by my bed and read it often. When I get to heaven, I shall make a point of finding George MacDonald, just to say thank you.

> I said, 'Let me walk in the fields.'
> He said, 'Nay, walk in the town.'
> I said, 'There are no flowers there.'
> He said, 'No flowers but a crown.'
>
> I said, 'But the sky is black,
> There is nothing but noise and din.'
> But He wept as He led me back.
> 'There is more,' He said, 'There is sin.'
>
> I said, 'But the air is thick
> And fogs are veiling the sun.'
> He announced, 'Yet hearts are sick,
> And souls in the dark undone.'
>
> I said, 'I shall miss the light,
> And friends will miss me they say.'
> He answered me, 'Choose tonight
> If I am to miss you or they.'
>
> I pleaded for time to be given.
> He said, 'Is it hard to decide?

It will not seem so in heaven
To have followed the steps of your guide.'

I cast one look at the fields
Then set my face to the town.
He said, 'My child, do you yield?
Will you leave the flowers for the crown?'

Then into His hand went mine
And into my heart came He,
And I walked in a light divine
The path I had feared to see.